Oh my stars!

THE JUNIOR LEAGUE *of*
ROANOKE VALLEY

★ ★ ★ ★ ★

Gives a Five-Star Salute to

The Assurance Company

for their generous assistance in
underwriting the cover of *Oh My Stars!*

Oh my stars!

Recipes that shine

Oh my stars!
Recipes that shine

Dedicated to the people of the Roanoke Valley, whose vibrance, warmth, humanity, and quest for the stars has provided a constant source of inspiration.

Photographer: Richard Boyd
Food Stylist: Jamie Nervo Cohan
Creative Director: David Hodge

Edited, Designed, and Manufactured by
Favorite Recipes® Press
an imprint of

FRP

P.O. Box 305142, Nashville, Tennessee 37230
800-358-0560

Art Director: Steve Newman
Editor: Jane Hinshaw

Library of Congress Catalog Number: 00-131126
ISBN: 0-9679497-0-X

Manufactured in the United States of America
First Printing: 2000   15,000 copies

Oh My Stars! includes recipes from
the League's earlier cookbook
Of Pots and Pipkins, denoted by

Foreword

There was a star danced, and under that I was born.
William Shakespeare
Much Ado About Nothing

Some stars may course the evening sky while others languish unseen in the heavens, but one star is firmly fixed to a 100-foot steel tower on a mountain 1,045 feet above Roanoke—the Mill Mountain Star, a National Historic Monument. It, alone among stars, is a manmade structure taller than an eight-story building, consisting of almost 2,000 feet of neon tubing. It is the most visible symbol of the Star City of the South.

Shortly after World War II, flushed with the hope engendered by postwar prosperity, the Roanoke Merchants Association conducted a campaign that raised more than $25,000 to construct a Christmas decoration celebrating the new peace and well-being. On Thanksgiving Eve of 1949, to great fanfare, Mayor A. R. Minton threw the inaugural switch. Since that night, without fail, the Mill Mountain Star has shone down upon Roanoke from dusk to midnight. On clear nights, it can be seen for a Roanoke forever.

It is our beacon. Under the star, nestled in the constant, yet ever-changing Blue Ridge Mountains, we educate a people, cultivate the arts, are nourished by nature's abundance, embrace history, look to the future, and take care of our own.

And yes, under the Star, we dance. We celebrate our gifts and our bounty. From intimate dinner parties, to simple family suppers, to sumptuous cocktail buffets, to children's birthday parties, to Parkway picnics, to a myriad of festivals throughout the Valley, we enjoy our lives and our food. Oh My Stars! seeks to share our celebration with you. We offer a glimpse of Roanoke through its cuisine, which is fresh, innovative, and elegant, but evocative of our past.

Table of Contents

Cookbook Committee

Co-Chairmen
Kelly Douthat
Martha Parrott

Marketing
Gray Lawson, Chairman
Jennifer Cotner
Laurie Gibbons
Kathryn Gurley
Marilyn Mullen-Harriman
Leigh Ann Myers
Ann Steadman
Tracey Thompson

Recipe and Tasting
Mary Catherine Baldridge, Chairman
Kate Robey, Assistant Chairman
Amanda Story, Secretary
Ann Belden
Christi Campbell
Pamela Clark
Paige Comer
Jennifer Murray
Amy Louise Reyer
Lisa Stanley
Lori Strauss
Leigh Thomas

Nonrecipe Text
Carolyn Bullington, Chairman
Suzanna Cory
Emily Henning
Jacqueline Kinder
Kit Rutherford

Art and Design
Gena Kepley, Chairman
Elizabeth Bush
Rebecca Doughton
Juliet Felts
Robyn Smeltzer

Mission Statement

The Junior League of Roanoke Valley, Virginia, Inc. is an organization of women committed to promoting voluntarism and improving the community through the effective action and leadership of trained volunteers. Its purpose is exclusively educational and charitable. The Association of Junior Leagues International, Inc. reaches out to women of all races, religious and national origins who demonstrate an interest in and commitment to voluntarism.

Vision Statement

The Junior League of Roanoke Valley, Virginia, Inc. has identified affordable child care as a critical need in our community and will work to improve the quality, affordability and accessibility through advocacy, education, fund-raising and working in partnership with existing programs and organizations.

Policy Statement

The Junior League of Roanoke Valley, Virginia, Inc. is committed to ensuring that children and their families have the opportunities and services for optimal physical, educational, cultural, emotional and social growth and development.

Therefore, be it resolved that the Junior League of Roanoke Valley, Virginia, Inc. has identified the welfare of children and their families as a critical need in our community and will work to improve the welfare of children through advocacy, education, fund-raising, and working in partnership with existing programs and organizations.

Introduction

In 1926 Mary Terry Goodwin Kuyk and her bridge club formed the nucleus of what is now the Junior League of Roanoke Valley. By 1930 they had opened a day nursery, joined the Association of Junior Leagues of America, opened a Summer Health School for underprivileged and undernourished children, and helped build and staff the Hospital Library and Roanoke Clinic.

Since then, the League has touched virtually every area of the cultural and community services landscape. During the Depression, League pioneers worked in tandem with other community groups to create the Council of Social Agencies, the Department of Public Welfare, and the Demonstration Casework Agency, later the Family Services Association.

The end of the Depression and the beginning of a world war signalled a new era for the League. Although contributing to the war effort consumed the bulk of the League's time and energy, the League also assisted in the opening of Community Children's Theater and a children's dramatic training school.

With peace, the League once again devoted itself to cultural and civic pursuits. Charity balls, fashion shows, and semiannual rummage sales helped fund the enormously popular Children's Theater and Story Time broadcasts as well as the Academy of Music, fine arts exhibits, the Roanoke Youth Symphony, the Teenage Girls Center, and Greenvale Nursery School.

League involvement in enriching the community has continued through drama programs; the Arts Festival; therapeutic arts programs; lectures and lawn concerts at Cherry Hill; the establishment of the Roanoke Valley Arts Council; historic tours; Great Books Projects; Explore Park; and the museums of art, science, and transportation.

The League has enhanced the social services network, as well. It has educated the public and played a key role in establishing Habitat, a group foster home for teenage girls; the Child Abuse and Neglect Coordinating Council; Ronald McDonald House; and the Volunteer Bureau.

Central to its volunteer efforts is improving the lot of the children of the Roanoke Valley, and the League has won national awards for an innovative program providing after-school care and tutoring to at-risk children. League volunteers have mentored families, taught life-skills courses to pregnant teens and teen mothers, and opened the door to the world of reading to elementary school students. League fund-raising efforts have contributed to community programs, schools, and daycare facilities.

The pride taken in this is unmistakable but understandable. In 1959 the League sponsored the first Harvest Bowl, an annual meeting of two Virginia college or university football teams, which raised more than $114,000 for League projects in its 15-year history. Jane Engleby, a League member who could well be speaking for all League successes, commented after the inaugural game, "Football may be a masculine domain, but it was a group of women who filled the stadium...it was a group of women who made $14,877 and brought Miss America to Roanoke. I think we could go to the men of our community now and say 'The Junior League is going to launch a missile' and they would not only back us—but they would volunteer to take the ride!" It would be a ride to the stars.

Starting Points

Appetizers & Beverages

The Hotel Roanoke

The Hotel Roanoke has graced Roanoke's landscape since 1882 when it became the centerpiece of the Norfolk and Western Railroad's plan to develop Big Lick into a major city. The hotel, ever the elegant and warm retreat to Roanokers, visitors, celebrities, and politicians alike, has built its excellent reputation with impeccable service from the first day.

The hotel is nationally renowned for hosting spectacular events, from unforgettable weddings to grand galas. The nostalgic Regency Room offers some of the valley's most delicious cuisines, including the hotel's signature Peanut Soup. The antique-filled lobby and the cozy Pine Room Pub present the hotel's rich history. The Conference Center, one of the top in the nation, offers the latest meeting technology, including ethernet access in all rooms. With well-appointed rooms, top-quality amenities, and award-winning service, The Hotel Roanoke and Conference Center holds a favorite place in the hearts of all who enjoy the facility.

Provisions Gourmet
Star Sponsor

Appetizers & Beverages

Antoinetta Bruschetta

2 tablespoons Dijon mustard
2 tablespoons olive oil
2 tablespoons red wine vinegar
2 cups chopped tomatoes
$1/2$ cup thinly sliced green onions
$1/2$ cup chopped green olives
garlic powder to taste
1 French baguette

Garnish
grated Parmesan cheese

Combine the mustard, olive oil and vinegar in a bowl. Add the tomatoes, green onions, olives and garlic powder. Marinate, covered, in the refrigerator for 30 minutes to 4 hours.

Cut the baguette into thin slices and place on a baking sheet. Broil just until lightly toasted.

Spread the tomato mixture on the toasted bread slices. Serve with Parmesan cheese to sprinkle over the top.

Makes three dozen

Bruschetta alla Pomodoro

To save calories, rub the bread slices with the garlic only, omitting the olive oil. You may also add feta cheese to the tomato mixture.

10 Roma tomatoes, coarsely chopped
$1/2$ onion, minced
4 garlic cloves, minced
2 tablespoons olive oil
10 fresh basil leaves, julienned
1 teaspoon minced fresh rosemary
salt and freshly ground pepper to taste
10 baguette slices
1 garlic clove, cut into halves
olive oil

Combine the tomatoes, onion, minced garlic cloves, 2 tablespoons olive oil, basil and rosemary in a bowl. Season with salt and pepper and mix well.

Rub the bread slices with the garlic halves and brush with additional olive oil. Arrange on a baking sheet or grill rack. Broil or grill until toasted. Spread with the tomato mixture.

Serves ten

Blue Ridge Parkway

In 1935, in the midst of the Great Depression, the Works Project Administration started construction of the Blue Ridge Parkway along the high peaks of the Blue Ridge and Great Smoky Mountains. This mammoth undertaking continued for more than 50 years and resulted in 469 miles of winding two-lane roads that are an engineering masterpiece.

Engineering masterpiece aside, the Parkway is visually spectacular. Sandstone and limestone ridges cloaked in oak, hornbeam, maple, hickory, tupelo, dogwood, and ash change moods with the seasons. Stately canopies of evergreens are ever constant, and mountain laurel and rhododendron provide a winsome leitmotif.

Designed for leisurely drives, the Parkway provides over 250 overlooks, leg-stretcher trails, tunnels, campgrounds, picnic areas, lodges, restaurants, old log cabins, and a Folk Art Center. Born of poverty, it brings a rich tranquility to those who travel it today.

★ Sidebar Stars

Mrs. J. Patrick Green
Mrs. Peter A. Leggett
Mrs. John H. Parrott
Mrs. Ward W. Stevens, Jr.

Grilled Chicken Bites with Red Pepper Pesto

Southerners use the term "pick-up" to describe finger food, and these are the perfect pick-up.

Red Pepper Pesto
1 (7-ounce) jar roasted red peppers, drained
1/2 cup fresh cilantro leaves
1 small garlic clove, chopped
6 tablespoons olive oil
3 tablespoons balsamic vinegar
1/2 teaspoon dry mustard
1/2 teaspoon ground coriander
1/8 teaspoon ground cinnamon
1/2 cup (2 1/2 ounces) whole toasted almonds
salt and pepper to taste

Chicken
4 boneless skinless chicken breasts
2 tablespoons olive oil
salt and pepper to taste

For the pesto, combine the roasted red peppers, cilantro, garlic, olive oil, vinegar, dry mustard, coriander and cinnamon in a food processor container. Process until puréed. Add the almonds and process until the almonds are finely chopped but not ground. Season with salt and pepper. Chill, covered, in the refrigerator for up to 2 days. Let stand at room temperature for 1 hour before serving.

For the chicken, heat a grill or broiler to medium-hot. Brush the chicken with olive oil and season with salt and pepper. Grill or broil on each side for 5 minutes or until cooked through.

Cut the chicken into 1-inch pieces. Place a wooden pick in each piece and arrange around the pesto on a serving plate.

Serves ten

Crab Meat Endive Spears

Exquisite presentation and combination of flavors make this a showstopper.

6 ounces crab meat, drained
1/2 cup frozen corn kernels, thawed
1/4 cup finely chopped red onion
1/4 cup mayonnaise
1 tablespoon thawed frozen orange juice concentrate
1 tablespoon fresh lemon juice
1 teaspoon grated lemon zest
4 teaspoons mixed chopped fresh herbs, such as tarragon, chervil and parsley
1/2 teaspoon ground cumin
1/4 teaspoon cayenne pepper, or to taste
2 heads Belgian endive

Garnish
1 tablespoon finely chopped fresh parsley
paprika to taste

Combine the crab meat with the corn, onion, mayonnaise, orange juice concentrate, lemon juice, lemon zest, mixed fresh herbs, cumin and cayenne pepper in a medium bowl and mix well. Chill, covered, in the refrigerator for up to 24 hours.

Separate the endive into leaves. Drain the crab meat mixture well and spoon 1 rounded tablespoon onto the base end of each leaf. Garnish with the parsley and paprika. Arrange on serving platters.

Serves ten

No-Holds Bar

The following is a guide to purchasing the correct quantities of each beverage and mixer for 75 guests. Take into account the preferences of your guests and the season and adjust the amounts accordingly. The list reflects the fact that southerners are notoriously big fans of bourbon.

4 liters Scotch
3 liters vodka
4 liters bourbon
3 liters gin
1 liter rum
1 liter tequila
3 cases Champagne
2 cases dry white wine
6 bottles dry red wine
750 milliliters vermouth
750 milliliters sherry
750 milliliters Dubonnet or Campari
1/2 case regular beer (more in the summer)
1 case light beer (more in the summer)
24 (5-ounce) bottles sparkling water
1 case tonic water
3 cases club soda or seltzer
24 (2-liter) bottles mixers
1 quart fruit juice
12 limes and 12 lemons
1 pitcher ice water
1 pound ice per person

Corn Quesadillas

1 (16-ounce) package frozen corn kernels, thawed
1/4 cup chopped jalapeño peppers
1 tablespoon oregano
ground cumin to taste
cayenne pepper to taste
olive oil
2 (10-count) packages flour tortillas
2 cups shredded sharp Cheddar, Swiss, mozzarella or Monterey Jack cheese

Sauté the corn with the jalapeño peppers, oregano, cumin and cayenne pepper in a small amount of olive oil in a skillet over medium-high heat for 10 to 15 minutes or until golden brown.

Heat a skillet brushed with olive oil and place 1 tortilla in the skillet. Top with some of the corn mixture, cheese and a second tortilla. Cook for 5 minutes or until brown on both sides, turning once. Remove to an ovenproof plate, cover with foil and keep warm in a 150-degree oven. Repeat with the remaining ingredients. Cut the quesadillas into quarters and serve with Chunky Guacamole (below).

Makes forty

Chunky Guacamole

1/4 cup chopped seeded tomato
2 tablespoons chopped onion
1/2 jalapeño pepper, seeded, chopped
2 teaspoons chopped fresh cilantro
2 teaspoons fresh lime juice
1 medium avocado, chopped
salt to taste

Combine the tomato, onion, jalapeño pepper, cilantro and lime juice in a small bowl and mix well. Add the avocado and salt and mix gently. Chill, covered, until serving time. Serve with tortilla chips.

Makes one and one-half cups

Curried Deviled Eggs

6 large eggs, hard-cooked
1 tablespoon minced green onions
1/4 cup mayonnaise
3/4 teaspoon curry powder
salt and pepper to taste

Garnish
1 tablespoon minced fresh parsley
niçoise olives

Cut the eggs into halves lengthwise. Scoop the yolks into a medium bowl and mash with a fork. Add the green onions, mayonnaise and curry powder and mix well. Season with salt and pepper.
Spoon or pipe the yolk mixture into the egg whites. Garnish with the parsley and olives.
Serves six

Lib Wilhelm's Pineapple Victoria

1 pineapple
1 cup sugar
1/3 cup water
1/4 cup Triple Sec
1/4 cup lime juice
grated zest of 1 orange

Cut the pineapple into halves lengthwise. Scoop out the pulp with a sharp knife, reserving the shells. Cut the pulp into bite-size pieces.
Combine the sugar and water in a small saucepan and bring to a boil, stirring to dissolve the sugar. Remove from the heat and add the Triple Sec, lime juice and orange zest and mix well. Combine with the chopped pineapple in a bowl. Cover the chopped pineapple and the reserved shells and chill for 8 hours or longer.
Spoon the marinated pineapple into the shells to serve.
Serves ten

Lib Wilhelm: Caterer to the Star

Lib Wilhelm is a local culinary legend, first as hostess and later as professional caterer. Lib's food has graced many a table, satisfied many a palate, and always stayed in tune with the times.

Although her star shines from brunch to dessert, her formula for a successful cocktail party for fifty is a lesson for any chef. Simply offer four or five choices on an exquisitely appointed table and supplement with two or three showstoppers passed on a tray.

Selecting Portobellos

When buying portobellos, look for those with a firm underside and lighter-colored gills. A gill area that appears very dark or spread out is a sign of age. To remove mushroom gills, hold the cap in one hand and gently scrape out the gills with a spoon. The thick, woody stems of these mushrooms can be reserved for stock or broth flavoring.

Simmered Mushrooms Bourguignonne

*4 pounds extra-large whole
    mushrooms
1 pound (4 sticks) butter
1 quart burgundy
2 cups boiling water
4 beef bouillon cubes
4 chicken bouillon cubes
1 1/2 tablespoons Worcestershire sauce
1 tablespoon MSG
1 teaspoon each dillweed and garlic powder
1 teaspoon freshly ground pepper
salt to taste*

Combine the mushrooms with the butter, wine, boiling water, bouillon cubes, Worcestershire sauce, MSG, dillweed, garlic powder and pepper in a large saucepan. Bring to a slow boil over medium heat. Reduce the heat and simmer, covered, for 5 to 6 hours. Cook, uncovered, for 3 to 5 hours or until the liquid is reduced enough to just cover the mushrooms. Season with salt.

Chill, covered, in the refrigerator until serving time. Reheat to serve from a chafing dish.

Serves twenty-five

Piccalilli

*2 1/2 pounds ground round
1 pound lean ground pork
3 large onions, finely chopped
5 or 6 large tomatoes, peeled, chopped
5 or 6 garlic cloves, finely chopped
3/4 (1-pound) package seedless raisins
1 small jar jalapeño peppers, drained, chopped
1 package almonds, chopped
1 tablespoon oregano
salt and cracked pepper to taste
1/2 cup flour*

Brown the ground round and ground pork with the onions in a saucepan, stirring until the ground beef and pork are crumbly and the onions are tender but not brown; drain. Add the tomatoes, garlic, raisins, jalapeño peppers, almonds, oregano, salt and pepper and mix well.

Simmer until the tomatoes are tender. Sprinkle with the flour. Cook until thickened, stirring constantly. Serve hot from a chafing dish with corn chip scoops.

Serves sixteen

Barbecued Shrimp

1 cup (2 sticks) butter
1 cup vegetable oil
1 tablespoon minced garlic
1 teaspoon lemon juice
4 dried bay leaves, finely crushed
1 tablespoon paprika
2 teaspoons rosemary
3/4 teaspoon dried basil
3/4 teaspoon oregano
1/2 teaspoon salt
1/2 teaspoon cayenne pepper
3/4 teaspoon black pepper
2 pounds large shrimp in shells

Melt the butter with the oil in a large cast-iron skillet and mix well. Add the garlic, lemon juice, bay leaves, paprika, rosemary, basil, oregano, salt, cayenne pepper and black pepper. Bring to a boil over medium heat, stirring constantly. Reduce the heat and simmer for 7 to 8 minutes, stirring frequently. Remove from the heat and let stand for 30 minutes or longer.

Add the shrimp to the mixture in the skillet. Cook over medium heat for 6 to 8 minutes or until the shrimp are pink and cooked through. Bake at 450 degrees for 10 minutes. Serve immediately with crusty French bread for dipping into the butter sauce.

Serves eight

Snap-Crackle-Pop Cheese Wafers

1 cup crisp rice cereal
1 cup shredded sharp Cheddar cheese
1 cup flour
1/2 cup (1 stick) butter
salt and red pepper to taste

Combine the cereal, cheese, flour, butter, salt and red pepper in a food processor and process until well mixed. Divide into 2 equal portions and roll into logs in waxed paper. Chill in the refrigerator for 1 hour or longer.

Cut the rolls into thin slices and arrange on baking sheets. Bake at 375 degrees for 10 minutes. Cool slightly on the baking sheets; remove to a wire rack to cool completely.

Makes three dozen

Flavored Ice Cubes

Adding flavored ice cubes to a favorite drink is a simple and festive way to enhance its flavor. Some suggestions are:

- *Lemonade frozen with edible flowers*

- *Puréed berries frozen with a mint leaf, lemon zest, or orange slice*

- *Coffee, to add to an iced latte, cappuccino, or macchiato*

- *Fresh cream frozen with a coffee bean, to add to iced coffee or Kahlúa*

- *Puréed watermelon, to add to a tequila sunrise or screwdriver*

- *Pineapple juice frozen with a mint leaf and coconut flakes, to add to a piña colada*

- *Tomato juice frozen with a touch of horseradish and basil chiffonade, to add to a Bloody Mary*

Pecans with a Punch

These could be called "Disappearing Pecans" because they go so quickly. They are excellent on the bar at a cocktail party.

1/2 cup sugar
1/4 cup Jack Daniel's Old No. 7 sour mash whiskey
1 teaspoon chili powder
1 teaspoon salt
3/4 teaspoon cayenne pepper
2 cups pecan halves

Combine the sugar, whiskey, chili powder, salt and cayenne pepper in a saucepan. Cook over medium heat until the sugar dissolves, stirring frequently. Bring to a boil and boil gently for 3 minutes, stirring occasionally.
Add the pecans, stirring to coat well. Spread in a single layer on a baking sheet lined with buttered foil. Bake at 250 degrees for 15 to 20 minutes or until toasted and glazed. Let stand until cool.
Serves six to eight

Artichoke and Spinach Dip

1 (16-ounce) can artichoke hearts, drained, chopped
1 (12-ounce) package frozen spinach soufflé, thawed
1 cup grated Parmesan cheese
1 cup shredded Monterey Jack cheese
1 cup shredded Monterey Jack cheese with jalapeño peppers
1 (16-ounce) jar medium salsa

Combine the artichoke hearts, spinach soufflé, Parmesan cheese and Monterey Jack cheeses in a bowl and mix well. Spoon into a baking dish. Bake at 350 degrees for 30 minutes. Top with the salsa and serve with tortilla chips.
Serves twelve

Black-Eyed Pea Dip

2 (16-ounce) cans black-eyed peas, drained
1 cup chopped green bell pepper
1/4 cup finely chopped onion
1/2 cup sliced green onions
1 or 2 jalapeño peppers, seeded, chopped
1 (4-ounce) jar chopped pimentos, drained
1 teaspoon garlic salt
pepper to taste
1/2 cup Italian salad dressing

Combine the black-eyed peas, bell pepper, onion, green onions, jalapeño peppers, pimentos, garlic salt and pepper in a bowl. Add the salad dressing and mix well. Chill until serving time. Serve with tortilla chips.

Serves twelve

California Dip

1 (10-ounce) can tomatoes with green chiles
2 fresh tomatoes, peeled, chopped
1 1/2 cups shredded Swiss cheese
1 1/2 cups shredded Monterey Jack cheese
2 bunches green onions, chopped
2 (4-ounce) cans chopped green chiles
2 (4-ounce) cans chopped black olives
1 tablespoon MSG
1 (8-ounce) bottle Italian salad dressing

Combine the tomatoes with green chiles, fresh tomatoes, Swiss cheese, Monterey Jack cheese, green onions, green chiles, black olives and MSG in a bowl. Add the salad dressing and mix well. Chill, covered, in the refrigerator for several hours. Serve with corn chip scoops.

Serves sixteen

Little Dippers

A little imagination can add new and exciting dimensions to dips. Choose an assortment of fresh vegetables or fruits with different textures and colors.

For vegetables, try asparagus spears, broccoli or cauliflower florets, carrot or celery sticks, cherry tomatoes, cucumber slices, blanched green beans, green onions, green or red pepper strips, jicama strips, mushrooms, radish roses, sugar snap peas, snow peas, turnip strips, or squash slices.

For fruits, try apple wedges, banana slices, cantaloupe or honeydew cubes, grapes, peach or pear slices, pineapple chunks, or strawberries.

Lib Wilhelm's French Bread Dip

1 (2-pound) round loaf French bread
12 ounces cream cheese
6 cups (1 1/2 pounds) shredded Monterey Jack cheese
1 1/2 green or red bell peppers, chopped
1 1/2 bunches green onions, chopped
1 1/2 (4-ounce) cans chopped green chiles
1 1/2 (3-ounce) packages dried beef, chopped
1 1/2 teaspoons onion powder
1 1/2 teaspoons chili powder
1 1/2 teaspoons cumin
1 1/2 teaspoons salt
1 1/2 teaspoons seasoned salt
1 1/2 teaspoons cayenne pepper
1 1/2 teaspoons white pepper
1 1/2 medium tomatoes, chopped

Cut the top from the bread and scoop out the center to form a shell; reserve the bread removed for another use.

Melt the cream cheese in a large saucepan over low heat. Add the Monterey Jack cheese and cook until melted, stirring to blend well. Add the bell peppers, green onions, green chiles and dried beef and mix well. Season with the onion powder, chili powder, cumin, salt, seasoned salt, cayenne pepper and white pepper, mixing well. Stir in the chopped tomatoes and remove from the heat. Let stand for several minutes.

Spoon the cheese mixture into the bread shell. Serve the dip warm or at room temperature with corn chip scoops. To reheat, wrap in plastic wrap and microwave until heated through.

Serves twenty

Oysters Rockefeller Dip

A Chesapeake classic.

1 cup finely chopped green onions
1/2 cup chopped green bell pepper
1/2 cup chopped celery
1/2 cup chopped parsley
1 cup thawed frozen spinach, drained
1/2 cup (1 stick) butter
1/2 cup bread crumbs
1 pint oysters, drained, chopped
1/8 teaspoon minced garlic
5 or 6 drops of hot pepper sauce
1/4 teaspoon salt
1/4 teaspoon pepper

Garnish
1/2 cup chopped lettuce

Sauté the green onions, bell pepper, celery, parsley and spinach in the butter in a medium skillet over medium heat for 5 minutes. Add the bread crumbs and oysters and mix well. Cook for 3 to 5 minutes. Stir in the garlic, hot sauce, salt and pepper. Cook for 5 minutes or until the oysters are cooked through.

Spoon into a chafing dish. Garnish with the lettuce and serve with toast points or melba rounds.

Serves twenty-four

Spicy Shrimp Salsa

1 pound large shrimp, peeled, deveined, cooked
2 Roma tomatoes, seeded, chopped
1/4 cup chopped red onion
1/2 serrano chile, seeded, minced
1/3 cup chopped fresh cilantro
1 tablespoon chopped fresh parsley
juice of 1 lime
1/4 cup olive oil
salt and freshly ground pepper to taste

Cut each shrimp into 4 or 5 pieces. Combine with the tomatoes, onion, serrano chile, cilantro and parsley in a medium bowl. Add the lime juice and olive oil and toss to mix well. Season with salt and pepper. Serve with tortilla chips.

Serves four to six

Variations: Mango, red onion, cilantro and mild green chiles; tomatoes, onion, herbs and unsalted peanuts; canned tomatillos, pineapple, onion, cilantro and orange juice; pineapple, yellow bell pepper, red onion and jalapeño peppers; corn kernels, red bell pepper, red onion, mango and cilantro; kiwifruit, red onion, cilantro and jalapeño peppers.

Roasted Sweet Potato Hummus

Gorgeous color and innovative ingredients make for a sure-fire hit.

3 cups chopped peeled sweet potatoes
2¹/2 cups chopped onions
1¹/2 cups chopped carrots
1 tablespoon olive oil
¹/4 cup tahini
¹/4 teaspoon salt
¹/8 teaspoon pepper

Combine the sweet potatoes, onions, carrots and olive oil in a large bowl and mix to coat well. Spread in a 10×15-inch roasting pan. Roast at 350 degrees for 1 hour or until the sweet potatoes are tender.

Combine the roasted vegetables with the tahini, salt and pepper in a food processor container and process until smooth. Serve with breadsticks or crackers.

Tahini, or sesame seed paste, can be found in most well-stocked markets.

Makes three cups

Sweet Onion and Cheddar Dip

3 large Vidalia onions, chopped
2 tablespoons unsalted butter
1 cup mayonnaise
2 cups shredded sharp Cheddar cheese
1 garlic clove, minced
¹/2 teaspoon Tabasco sauce

Sauté the onions in the butter in a skillet until tender; drain. Combine with the mayonnaise, cheese, garlic and Tabasco sauce in a bowl and mix well.

Spoon into a buttered baking dish. Bake at 375 degrees for 25 minutes. Serve with tortilla chips or crackers.

Serves twelve to fifteen

Sun-Dried Tomato and Roasted Pepper Dip

8 sun-dried tomato halves
2 (7-ounce) jars roasted red peppers
1 garlic clove, minced
salt to taste
2 tablespoons chopped flat-leaf parsley
1 tablespoon fresh lemon juice
4 ounces cream cheese, chopped, softened
1/2 cup sour cream
pepper to taste

Garnish
chopped flat-leaf parsley

Soak the sun-dried tomatoes in enough hot water to cover for 5 minutes; drain and pat dry. Drain the peppers and pat dry. Mash the garlic with salt to taste in a small bowl.

Combine the garlic paste, peppers, tomatoes, parsley and lemon juice in a food processor container and process until puréed.

Add the cream cheese and sour cream and season to taste with salt and pepper; process until smooth, scraping the side of the container occasionally. Spoon into a serving bowl and garnish with additional parsley. Serve with toasted pita triangles or crudités.

Makes two and one-half cups

Roasted Red Pepper Pimento Cheese

1 cup chopped roasted red pepper
1 cup chopped pimentos
5 cups (1 1/4 pounds) shredded sharp white New York or
    Vermont Cheddar cheese
1/4 cup grated Parmesan cheese
1/4 cup stuffed green olives, finely chopped
1 tablespoon chopped fresh parsley
1/2 cup mayonnaise
cayenne pepper to taste
1/2 teaspoon freshly ground black pepper

Combine the roasted red pepper, pimentos, Cheddar cheese, Parmesan cheese, green olives and parsley in a bowl. Add the mayonnaise, cayenne pepper and black pepper and mix well. Chill, covered, until serving time.

Makes two and one-half cups

How To Roast Peppers

Coat bell peppers lightly with olive oil and place on a baking sheet. Roast at 500 degrees on the top oven rack for 25 minutes or until blistered and charred in places, turning once or twice. Place in a plastic bag or small bowl. Seal the bag or cover the bowl tightly with plastic wrap. Let stand for 10 to 15 minutes or until the skins can be easily removed. Peel and chop, discarding the seeds.

Mill Mountain Zoo

A Siberian tiger named Ruby makes her home behind the Star. In the enchanted woods atop Mill Mountain she joins red pandas, snow leopards, tree kangaroos, and more than fifty other species of exotic and native animals.

Since 1952, Roanokers have known these precious ten acres as the Mill Mountain Zoo, where they can meander along the zoo's secluded pathways and observation areas while visiting with the animals. Children can take a ride on the Zoo Choo or visit the education area, better known as Camp Wildcat, where they can learn through hands-on exhibits and interact with small animals. During the summer, events take place regularly in the zoo's amphitheater. Special programming, some of which has become ritual to the children of the Roanoke Valley, is scheduled throughout the year.

★ *Sidebar Stars*
Janet and Jim Frantz

Lib Wilhelm's Cheese Slaw

1 pound Swiss cheese, coarsely shredded
1 bunch green onions with tops, chopped
1/2 cup chopped mild banana peppers
1/2 cup finely chopped jalapeño peppers
mayonnaise
1 head cabbage

Combine the cheese, green onions, banana peppers and jalapeño peppers in a bowl. Add enough mayonnaise to bind and mix well. Store in the refrigerator for up to 1 week. Add additional mayonnaise if needed at serving time.

Hollow out the center of the cabbage and fold back the outer leaves. Spoon the cheese mixture into the center. Serve with corn chip scoops.

Serves sixteen

Mill Mountain Cheese Spread

8 ounces cream cheese, softened
1 garlic clove, minced
1 tablespoon grated onion
1/4 cup (1/2 stick) butter
1/4 cup packed dark brown sugar
1 teaspoon Worcestershire sauce
1/2 teaspoon prepared mustard
1 cup finely chopped pecans

Combine the cream cheese, garlic and onion in a bowl and mix with a fork. Shape into a 6-inch circle with a raised rim on a serving plate. Chill, covered, in the refrigerator.

Combine the butter, brown sugar, Worcestershire sauce, mustard and pecans in a saucepan and cook until the butter melts, stirring to mix well. Spoon over the cream cheese mixture. Chill, covered, in the refrigerator. Let return to room temperature and serve with crackers.

Serves ten to twelve

Savory Herbed Cheesecake

Lemon Crust
1 cup flour
$^1/2$ cup (1 stick) butter, cut into tablespoons
finely grated zest of 1 lemon
$^1/2$ teaspoon salt
3 tablespoons lemon juice
1 egg yolk

Filling
24 ounces cream cheese, softened
3 tablespoons flour
4 large eggs
2 tablespoons lemon juice
1 cup grated Parmigiano-Reggiano cheese
4 shallots, finely chopped
$^1/2$ cup chopped parsley
1 tablespoon chopped fresh basil, or 1 teaspoon dried basil
$1^1/2$ teaspoons chopped fresh oregano, or $^1/2$ teaspoon dried oregano
$1^1/2$ teaspoons chopped fresh tarragon, or $^1/2$ teaspoon dried tarragon
1 teaspoon minced fresh rosemary, or $^1/3$ teaspoon dried rosemary
$^1/2$ teaspoon hot pepper sauce
1 teaspoon salt

Garnish
3 large tomatoes
3 basil sprigs

For the crust, process the flour, butter, lemon zest and salt in a food processor for several seconds. Add the lemon juice and egg yolk and pulse just until well mixed. Press $^1/3$ of the mixture over the bottom of an 8- or 9-inch springform pan sprayed with nonstick cooking spray; press the remaining crumb mixture up the side. Chill in the freezer.

For the filling, process the cream cheese in a food processor until smooth. Add the flour and 1 of the eggs and process until well mixed; scrape the side of the container. Add the remaining 3 eggs 1 at a time, processing until smooth after each addition. Add the lemon juice, Parmigiano-Reggiano cheese, shallots, parsley, basil, oregano, tarragon, rosemary, pepper sauce and salt and process just until well mixed.

Spoon the filling into the prepared crust. Bake at 400 degrees for 15 minutes. Reduce the oven temperature to 325 degrees and bake for 50 minutes longer or until golden brown. Cool on a wire rack for 10 minutes. Loosen from the side of the pan with a thin knife and place on a serving plate; remove the side of the pan. Cool at room temperature for 1 hour before serving or store in the refrigerator for up to 2 days and return to room temperature to serve.

For the garnish, peel each tomato in 1 long strip. Wind each strip into a rose shape and arrange on the top of the cheesecake. Add basil sprig leaves.

To serve, cut an inner circle about $1^1/2$ inches from the edge and cut into $^3/4$-inch slices.

Serves fifteen to twenty

The Homestead

Since 1766, the Homestead has offered visitors an incomparable retreat and incredibly grand escape amidst the beauty of Virginia's Allegheny Mountains. More than 500 luxuriously appointed rooms and suites, superb dining, exquisite shopping, and traditional Southern hospitality at its finest await lucky visitors.

The Homestead is 15,000 acres of relaxation and recreation for the whole family. Visitors may choose from three premier golf courses—including the acclaimed Cascades Course—as well as a renowned spa and salon, horseback and carriage rides, shooting sports, hiking, biking, canoeing, bowling, skiing, and ice skating.

Whether dancing to the nightly orchestra, relaxing in one of the hotel's front porch rocking chairs, or sitting by a cozy fire at tea time, visitors will find this vacation escape is truly unforgettable.

Caramelized Onion and Gorgonzola Tart

A hearty starter on cold nights.

1 tablespoon butter
1 tablespoon olive oil
4 yellow or white onions, thinly sliced
1/2 cup sherry
1/2 cup cream
2 egg yolks
2 ounces Gorgonzola cheese, grated
chopped fresh thyme to taste
freshly cracked pepper to taste
1 recipe (2-crust) tart pastry, or 2 frozen pie shells, thawed

Melt the butter with the olive oil in a saucepan. Add the onions and cook over low heat until light brown. Stir in the sherry. Combine the cream, egg yolks, cheese, thyme and pepper in a mixing bowl and mix well.

Spread the onions in a pastry-lined tart pan. Pour the cheese mixture over the onions. Top with the remaining pastry; seal the edge and cut steam vents. Bake at 400 degrees for 30 minutes or until golden brown. Sprinkle with fresh thyme.

Serves eight

Italian Cheese Terrine

Sun-Dried Tomato Sauce
1 (15-ounce) can whole tomatoes
3/4 cup chopped onion
1 tablespoon finely chopped garlic
2 tablespoons olive oil
1/2 teaspoon sugar
2 bay leaves
1/4 teaspoon dried basil
1 (7-ounce) jar oil-pack sun-dried tomatoes, drained, chopped

Terrine
2 tablespoons butter, softened
8 ounces cream cheese, softened
2 tablespoons prepared pesto
1/2 cup grated Parmesan cheese
9 (1-ounce) slices mozzarella cheese

Garnish
fresh basil sprigs

For the sauce, drain the canned tomatoes, reserving 1/4 cup of the juice; chop the tomatoes. Sauté the onion and garlic in the olive oil in a large skillet over medium heat until tender. Add the canned tomatoes, sugar, bay leaves, basil and reserved tomato juice. Bring to a boil and reduce the heat. Simmer for 3 to 5 minutes or until thickened, stirring frequently. Remove from the heat and discard the bay leaves. Stir in the sun-dried tomatoes. Chill, covered, for 2 hours or longer.

For the terrine, beat the butter and cream cheese at medium speed in a mixing bowl until light. Add the pesto and Parmesan cheese and beat until smooth.

Line a 3-cup bowl or mold with plastic wrap, allowing 8 inches to hang over the edge. Cut 5 slices of the mozzarella cheese diagonally into halves. Line the bowl with the triangular slices, overlapping slightly. Cut the remaining mozzarella cheese into halves crosswise.

Layer the cream cheese mixture, tomato sauce and remaining mozzarella cheese slices 1/2 at a time in the prepared bowl. Fold the plastic wrap over the top and place a weight on top to press the layers. Chill for 8 hours to 3 days.

Peel the plastic wrap from the top of the terrine and invert onto a serving platter; remove the plastic wrap. Garnish with sprigs of basil and serve with crackers or melba rounds.

Serves sixteen

Lime Tea

5 tea bags
5 cups boiling water
1 (6-ounce) can frozen limeade concentrate, thawed
1 cup sugar
5 cups cold water

Garnish
lime slices
mint leaves

Steep the tea bags in the boiling water in a pitcher for 5 minutes; discard the tea bags. Add the limeade concentrate and sugar; mix well. Add the cold water and mix well. Serve over ice. Garnish with lime slices and mint.
Serves eight to ten

Adults-Only Orange Slush

Start off a summer luncheon with this refreshing drink. Serve in Jefferson cups with a spoon.

2 tea bags
1 cup boiling water
4 cups cold water
1 cup sugar
1 (6-ounce) can frozen lemonade concentrate, thawed
1 (6-ounce) can frozen orange juice concentrate, thawed
1 cup bourbon

Steep the tea bags in the boiling water in a bowl; discard the tea bags. Add the cold water, sugar, lemonade concentrate and orange juice concentrate and mix well. Stir in the bourbon. Freeze for 24 hours.
Serves eight

After-Dinner Delight

Pour into decorative bottles for a lovely holiday gift.

1 (14-ounce) can sweetened condensed milk
1 cup heavy cream
egg substitute equivalent to 4 eggs
2 tablespoons chocolate syrup
2 teaspoons instant coffee granules
1 teaspoon vanilla extract
1/2 teaspoon almond extract
1 3/4 cups Irish whiskey

Combine the condensed milk, cream, egg substitute, chocolate syrup, coffee granules and flavorings in a bowl and mix well. Stir in the whiskey. Store in an airtight container in the refrigerator for up to 1 month.
Makes five cups

Blackberry Margaritas

1 quart fresh blackberries
3/4 cup fresh lime juice
3/4 cup sugar
2 1/4 cups tequila
2 cups ice

Garnish
lime slices

Purée the blackberries in a food processor or blender. Strain and return the liquid to the food processor container. Add the lime juice, sugar, tequila and ice and process until smooth.
Pour into glasses and garnish with the lime slices.
Serves twelve

Bunco Night

What do the Wild Women of North Platte and the Whine and Wine Ladies have in common? They, along with thousands of women throughout this country and others, are caught in the grips of a nineteenth-century dice game known as Bunco. The rules are simple, if inconsistent, and anyone seeking to learn more about the game can visit the official Bunco website; read Maite G. Francke's discursive study, Sisterhood of Bunco: A Comprehensive Guide to the Game; *or go on a Bunco cruise.*

Bunco is, more than anything, social. Groups typically consist of twelve players who take turns being the hostess. If, as Coco Chanel once said, women dress for other women, then it follows that women entertain for other women as well. On this evening our homes are immaculate, our children are impeccably behaved, our husbands are dutiful, and our menus are inspired.

One Roanoke hostess, a recent emigre from Texas, at an introductory game served up Blackberry Margaritas, cold Coronas, Spicy Shrimp Salsa, and shortcake with strawberries the size of Dallas for dessert. Roanoke ladies have been rolling ever since.

The History of "The Drink"

One of the most requested drinks of the twentieth century came about as a result of different cultures and tastes colliding during the holiday season of 1947. An American couple, a Mr. and Mrs. Sames, was spending the Christmas season in Acapulco at their vacation home, where they frequently entertained. Mrs. Sames favored the local drink of tequila with lime juice, but she also greatly enjoyed Cointreau, an orange liqueur from France. During one particularly festive evening, she experimented by combining equal parts of the two, mixing Cointreau with tequila and lime juice and serving it over ice. It was instantly dubbed "The Drink." It remained such a hit that the following Christmas Mr. Sames gave his wife long-stemmed crystal glasses with shallow flat bowls for serving "The Drink." Into each glass had been etched the name of the inventor, his dear wife Margarita. Thus "The Drink" had a new name and the world, a new drink.

Creamy Coffee Frappé

*1 gallon triple-strength brewed coffee, cooled
5 gallons vanilla ice cream, softened
1 quart heavy cream
2 cups sugar
cinnamon to taste*

Combine the coffee, ice cream, cream and sugar in a large container and mix well. Chill, covered, for 30 minutes. Spoon into a punch bowl and sprinkle with cinnamon.

You may make the coffee with 1 gallon of boiling water and one 3-ounce jar of instant coffee granules if desired.

Serves one hundred to one hundred and fifty

Old-Fashioned Eggnog

*16 egg yolks
1 cup sugar
16 egg whites
2 cups bourbon
1/2 cup light or dark rum
2 quarts half-and-half
2 cups whipping cream*

Garnish
grated nutmeg

Beat the egg yolks with the sugar in a large mixing bowl until thick and pale yellow. Beat the egg whites in a mixing bowl until stiff peaks form. Fold into the egg yolk mixture.

Add the bourbon and rum very gradually, stirring constantly. Stir in the half-and-half. Chill, covered, for several hours.

Whip the cream in a mixing bowl until soft peaks form. Skim the foam from the top of the egg mixture. Fold in the whipped cream gradually. Chill for 24 hours for a smoother texture. Garnish servings with nutmeg.

Serves thirty

Hot and Spicy Bloody Marys

Delicious served chilled, but also good served hot in a mug.

4 cups (1 quart) tomato juice
1/2 cup fresh lemon juice
1/2 cup beef broth
2 tablespoons prepared horseradish
Worcestershire sauce to taste
Tabasco sauce to taste
freshly ground pepper to taste
1 1/2 cups vodka

Garnish
8 celery ribs

Combine the tomato juice, lemon juice, beef broth, horseradish, Worcestershire sauce, Tabasco sauce and pepper in a saucepan. Bring to a simmer and simmer for 5 to 6 minutes to blend the flavors. Cool to room temperature.

Pour 3 tablespoons vodka over ice in each of 8 tall glasses. Fill with the tomato juice mixture and stir to mix well. Garnish with the celery ribs.

Serves eight

Vodka Buckets

26 ounces vodka
2 (6-ounce) cans frozen lemonade concentrate, thawed
2 (6-ounce) cans frozen limeade concentrate, thawed
2 (32-ounce) bottles lemon-lime soda, chilled

Garnish
mint sprigs

Combine the vodka, lemonade concentrate and limeade concentrate in a large container; mix well. Chill until serving time. Add the lemon-lime soda at serving time and mix gently. Serve in glasses with sugared rims. Garnish with mint sprigs.

Serves twelve to sixteen

Starlite Express
Soups & Salads

The Railroad

Roanoke was first and foremost a railroad town, and, in fact, traces its charter to the rails. In 1881, a group of Philadelphia entrepreneurs chose a spot known as Big Lick, later renamed Roanoke, as the headquarters for a new railroad—the Norfolk and Western. The rest is the history of a community.

Roanoke's humble beginnings as a railroad town provided the impetus for the construction of the Virginia Museum of Transportation, located in the historic freight station. It houses the largest collection of diesel locomotives in the South, significant collections of American carriages and automobiles, the photographic collection of the Association of American Railroads, and the Resource Library and Archives, the most extensive such resource library on the East Coast.

Of particular importance in the collection is the renowned N&W Class J Locomotive No. 611 and the Illinois Terminal "President 1" Business Car. This luxuriously appointed car—equipped with separate living and dining areas, three individual bedrooms, a shower, observation deck, stewards' quarters, kitchen, and pantry— was designed for use by the railroad's president.

Roanoke Electric Steel Corporation
Star Sponsor

Soups & Salads

Chilled Tomato Soup with Avocado Cream

Elegant, refined, and refreshing.

Soup
> 2 cups chopped onions
> 3/4 cup chopped carrots
> 1 tablespoon crushed garlic
> 1/4 cup canola oil
> 4 cups chicken broth
> 1 teaspoon salt
> 1/4 to 1/2 teaspoon cayenne pepper
> 4 pounds tomatoes, peeled, seeded, chopped, or
>   2 (28-ounce) cans chopped tomatoes, drained

Avocado Cream
> 2 very ripe avocados, chopped
> 2/3 cup sour cream
> 1/4 cup heavy cream
> 4 teaspoons lemon juice
> 1/2 teaspoon salt

Garnish
> chopped scallions

For the soup, sauté the onions, carrots and garlic in the heated oil in a large saucepan over medium heat for 15 minutes or until tender. Stir in the chicken broth, salt and cayenne pepper. Simmer for 30 minutes. Increase the heat and add the tomatoes. Cook for 10 minutes longer.

Purée the mixture in batches in a food processor. Combine in a bowl and cover. Chill for up to 24 hours.

For the avocado cream, combine the avocados, sour cream, cream, lemon juice and salt in a food processor container and process until smooth. Spoon into a bowl and chill, covered, until serving time.

To serve, ladle the soup into chilled soup bowls and spoon 1 or 2 tablespoons of the avocado cream over the top. Garnish with scallions.

Serves eight

Pilgrims at Tinker Mountain

Hollins University, historically a women's college, is located in the serene outskirts of Roanoke. Hollins is home to an internationally renowned creative writing program and claims Margaret Wise Brown and Annie Dillard as her own. When Dillard later returned to Roanoke to recuperate from pneumonia, she found repose along the banks of Tinker Creek. She chronicled her visits to the creek, and, in 1975, her gentle ruminations, published under the title Pilgrim at Tinker Creek, *won the Pulitzer Prize for nonfiction.*

Every fall, on a crisp October day, Hollins undergraduates awake to the pealing of church bells heralding Tinker Day—a day of good fellowship, good food, and no classes. Students start the day with fresh doughnuts, then costume themselves in the most tacky and bizarre conglomerations and hike up Tinker Mountain.

There, these pilgrims enjoy the panoramic view along with fried chicken, beans, and the traditional Tinker Cake served by the seniors. Skits add the final note to a memorable day and a lifelong memory.

★ *Sidebar Stars*
Ginny and Shields Jarrett

Fresh Berry Soup

Mix enough yogurt, buttermilk and sour cream together to measure 4 cups. Combine with 4 cups fresh orange juice, 2 tablespoons fresh lemon juice or lime juice and 1 or more tablespoons honey in a bowl. Add cinnamon and nutmeg to taste and mix well. Chill, covered, until serving time. Spoon 1¹/2 pints fresh raspberries, blueberries or sliced strawberries into 4 to 6 serving bowls and ladle the soup over the berries. Garnish with fresh mint.

Broccoli and Mushroom Soup

Just add two chopped cooked chicken breasts for a heartier main-dish version of this soup.

1 bunch broccoli, chopped
1 pound mushrooms, chopped
1 large onion, chopped
³/4 cup (1¹/2 sticks) butter
¹/2 cup flour
6 chicken bouillon cubes, crushed
1 teaspoon nutmeg
¹/2 teaspoon salt
1 teaspoon pepper
1 (14-ounce) can chicken broth
¹/2 cup water
4 cups half-and-half

Sauté the broccoli, mushrooms and onion in ¹/4 cup of the butter in a large saucepan.

Melt the remaining ¹/2 cup butter in a small saucepan. Stir in the flour, bouillon cubes, nutmeg, salt and pepper. Cook until bubbly, stirring constantly. Add to the broccoli mixture.

Stir in the chicken broth and water. Add the half-and-half gradually, stirring constantly. Cook over medium heat for 1 hour.

Serves six

Wertz's Country Store's Vermont Cheddar Soup

1 medium onion, chopped
2 ribs celery, chopped
1 medium carrot, chopped
6 tablespoons (³/4 stick) butter
¹/4 cup flour
4 cups chicken stock
8 ounces Vermont sharp Cheddar cheese, shredded
1 teaspoon dry or prepared mustard
1 cup half-and-half
salt, cayenne pepper and black pepper to taste

Sauté the onion, celery and carrot in the butter in a saucepan over medium heat for 3 minutes. Sprinkle with the flour and cook until bubbly, stirring constantly. Add the chicken stock 1 cup at a time, stirring constantly. Bring to a boil and reduce the heat. Simmer for 40 minutes.

Remove from the heat and add the cheese, mustard, half-and-half, salt, cayenne pepper and black pepper. Stir until the cheese melts and the mixture is smooth.

Serves eight

Hotel Roanoke's Peanut Soup

The hotel's signature soup has been a favorite of locals and travelers for many generations.

1 small onion, chopped
2 ribs celery, chopped
¹/2 cup (1 stick) butter
3 tablespoons flour
8 cups (2 quarts) chicken broth
2 cups peanut butter
1 tablespoon lemon juice
¹/3 teaspoon celery salt
1 teaspoon salt
¹/2 cup ground peanuts

Sauté the onion and celery in the butter in a saucepan for 5 minutes or until tender but not brown. Stir in the flour and cook until bubbly. Add the chicken broth. Cook until slightly thickened, stirring constantly. Cook for 30 minutes, stirring occasionally.

Strain the mixture into a second saucepan. Add the peanut butter, lemon juice, celery salt and salt and mix well. Cook just until heated through, stirring to blend well. Ladle into soup bowls and sprinkle with the ground peanuts. Serve with Hotel Roanoke's Spoonbread (page 135).

Serves ten

Simply Smashing Pumpkins and Other Souper Ideas

Turn your harvest into an enchanted evening by serving stew or soup in sugar pumpkins instead of ordinary bowls. There is no cleanup and guests enjoy a new spin on an old favorite.

Simply purchase small sugar pumpkins and carve a lid from the top of each one. Remove the seeds, rub the insides with olive oil and sprinkle with salt and pepper. Arrange the pumpkins and lids on parchment-lined baking sheets. Bake for 1 hour or until tender but still firm, turning after 30 minutes. Fill with the soup or stew and bake for 15 minutes longer or until the soup is heated through.

You can also hollow out small round loaves of bread. Brush inside and out with olive oil and toast in a 350-degree oven for about 10 minutes. Fill with the soup and serve immediately.

Butternut Squash Soup

An autumn favorite with a rich taste that belies the fact that there is very little added fat.

2$^1/_2$ to 3 pounds butternut squash
2 cups chopped onions
3 garlic cloves, chopped
1 (3-inch) piece gingerroot
2 tablespoons olive oil
1 teaspoon curry powder
$^1/_4$ teaspoon cinnamon
2 teaspoons salt
$^1/_4$ teaspoon pepper
4 cups chicken stock or water

Garnish
chopped fresh cilantro

Cut the squash into halves lengthwise, discarding the seeds. Place cut side down on a foil-lined baking sheet. Bake at 425 degrees for 1 hour or until tender. Cool slightly.

Sauté the onions, garlic and gingerroot in the heated olive oil in a large saucepan for 10 minutes or until tender but not brown. Stir in the curry powder, cinnamon, salt and pepper. Cook over low heat for 10 minutes, stirring constantly. Stir in the chicken stock. Bring to a boil and reduce the heat.

Scoop the squash pulp from the shells and add to the soup. Simmer for 20 minutes; discard the gingerroot. Purée the soup in batches in a blender. Combine in the saucepan and simmer until heated through. Ladle into soup bowls and garnish with cilantro.

You may prepare the soup several days in advance and store in the refrigerator; reheat to serve.

Serves four to six

Pumpkin and Black Bean Soup

The pumpkin adds great flavor and depth to a soup loaded with nutrients.

3 (15-ounce) cans black beans, rinsed, drained
1 cup drained canned tomatoes, chopped
1¹/₄ cups chopped onions
¹/₂ cup minced shallots
4 garlic cloves, minced
5 teaspoons ground cumin
1 teaspoon salt
¹/₂ teaspoon freshly ground pepper
¹/₄ cup (¹/₂ stick) unsalted butter
4 cups beef broth
1 (16-ounce) can pumpkin
¹/₂ cup dry sherry
8 ounces cooked ham, cut into ¹/₈-inch pieces
3 to 4 tablespoons sherry vinegar
salt and freshly ground pepper to taste

Garnish
sour cream
coarsely chopped pumpkin seeds, lightly toasted

Process the black beans and tomatoes in a food processor until coarsely puréed.

Sauté the onions, shallots, garlic, cumin, 1 teaspoon salt and ¹/₂ teaspoon pepper in the butter in a heavy 6-quart saucepan over medium heat until the onion is tender and begins to brown. Stir in the bean and tomato purée, beef broth, pumpkin and wine. Simmer for 25 minutes or until thick enough to coat the back of the spoon, stirring occasionally.

Add the ham and vinegar and simmer just until heated through. Season with salt and pepper to taste. Ladle into soup bowls and garnish with sour cream and pumpkin seeds.

Serves eight

Farmer's Market Vegetable Soup

A lively and vibrant melange.

2 (10-ounce) cans tomatoes with green chiles
2 large yellow squash, chopped
2 large zucchini, chopped
1 red onion, chopped
1 bunch scallions, chopped
1 tablespoon minced garlic
$^1/_4$ cup chopped fresh cilantro
$^1/_2$ cup uncooked quick-cooking brown rice
5 (14-ounce) cans vegetable broth
$1^1/_2$ cups water

Garnish
sour cream
2 avocados, chopped
freshly grated Parmesan cheese

Combine the tomatoes, yellow squash, zucchini, onion, scallions, garlic, cilantro, rice, vegetable broth and water in a large saucepan. Bring to a boil and reduce the heat. Simmer for $1^1/2$ to 2 hours or until of the desired consistency. Ladle into soup bowls and garnish with sour cream, avocados and Parmesan cheese.
Serves eight to ten

Sweet Yellow Pepper Soup with Crab Meat

Golden peppers combine with crab meat in this gorgeous soup.

6 yellow bell peppers, sliced
$1^1/2$ cups (or more) cream
salt and pepper to taste
4 ounces backfin crab meat

Combine the bell peppers with the cream in a heavy saucepan. Simmer for 15 minutes or until tender. Purée the mixture in a food processor. Strain into the saucepan and season with salt and pepper. Add the crab meat and cook just until heated through.
Serves four

Creamy Crab and Corn Chowder

1/2 cup chopped celery
1/2 cup chopped green onions
1/4 cup chopped green bell pepper
1/2 cup (1 stick) butter
2 (10-ounce) cans cream of potato soup
1 (17-ounce) can cream-style corn
1 1/2 cups half-and-half
1 1/2 cups milk
hot sauce to taste
2 bay leaves
1 teaspoon dried thyme leaves
1/2 teaspoon garlic powder
1/4 teaspoon white pepper
1 pound lump crab meat

Garnish
chopped parsley
lemon slices

Sauté the celery, green onions and green pepper in the butter in a heavy saucepan. Add the potato soup, corn, half-and-half, milk, hot sauce, bay leaves, thyme, garlic powder and white pepper; mix well. Cook until heated through.

Add the crab meat and mix gently. Cook until heated through; discard the bay leaves. Ladle into soup bowls and garnish with parsley and lemon slices.

Serves eight

The Finishing Touch

By garnishing a bowl of soup, the chef can add a contrasting flavor or texture, or simply improve the visual appeal of the dish.

Some attractive and easy garnishes include toasted shredded coconut, chopped peppers, shredded cheese, crumbled bacon, chopped fresh herbs, thinly sliced fruits or blanched vegetables, capers, chopped nuts, or crushed chips.

For a decorative garnish that is quite simple, pipe or drizzle sour cream over the surface of the soup and swirl through it with a wooden pick.

Montano's Lobster Bisque

3 (16-ounce) cans lobster
10 tablespoons (1 1/4 sticks) unsalted butter
1/4 cup flour
1 1/2 teaspoons finely ground sea salt
1/2 teaspoon cayenne pepper
2 quarts half-and-half
1/4 cup sherry

Drain the lobster, reserving the liquid. Chop the lobster coarsely and combine
with the reserved liquid and butter in a heavy saucepan. Cook over low heat for
several minutes. Stir in the flour, sea salt and cayenne pepper. Cook for 10 minutes,
stirring constantly.

Heat the half-and-half in a saucepan just until the surface begins to film. Add
to the lobster mixture with the sherry. Cook over low heat for 10 minutes, stirring
frequently; the mixture will scorch easily. Serve immediately or cool for 30 minutes and
store in the refrigerator and reheat to serve.

Serves twelve

Outstanding Oyster Stew

1 quart oysters
2 or 3 ribs celery, chopped
1 medium onion, chopped
1/4 cup (1/2 stick) butter
2 (4-ounce) cans chopped mushrooms
1/4 cup flour
1 cup white wine
2 teaspoons instant chicken bouillon
2 1/2 cups heavy cream
2 to 3 tablespoons grated Parmesan cheese
juice of 1/2 lemon
2 tablespoons chopped fresh parsley
thyme, nutmeg and pepper to taste

Drain the oysters, reserving the liquid. Sauté the celery and onion in the butter in
a saucepan. Add the mushrooms and simmer for several minutes. Stir in the flour. Cook
until bubbly. Add the wine, reserved oyster liquid and instant bouillon. Bring to a boil
and cook until thickened, stirring constantly.

Reduce the heat and stir in the cream, cheese, lemon juice, parsley, thyme, nutmeg
and pepper. Cook until heated through; do not boil. Add the oysters and cook just until
the edges curl. Serve immediately.

Serves eight to twelve

Chicken Chili with White Beans

Serve this variation on a traditional chili just as it is for a family dinner, or with the suggested garnishes for a festive occasion.

1 pound dried Great Northern white beans
5¼ cups chicken broth
1 large white onion, chopped
2 garlic cloves, minced
1 tablespoon dried oregano
1 tablespoon ground cumin
½ teaspoon ground cloves
1 teaspoon salt
1 tablespoon freshly ground white pepper
5 cups chopped cooked chicken breasts
1 (7-ounce) can chopped green chiles
1 tablespoon minced jalapeño peppers (optional)
1¾ cups chicken broth
8 flour tortillas

Garnish
shredded Monterey Jack cheese
sour cream
sliced black olives
chopped avocado
chunky salsa

Sort the beans. Soak the beans in water to cover in a large bowl for 8 hours; drain. Combine with 5¼ cups chicken broth, onion, garlic, oregano, cumin, cloves, salt and white pepper in a large saucepan. Simmer, covered, for 5 hours or until the beans are tender, stirring occasionally.

Add the chicken, green chiles, jalapeño peppers and 1¾ cups chicken broth. Simmer, covered, for 1 hour. Ladle into bowls lined with the tortillas. Serve with the cheese, sour cream, black olives, avocado and salsa for garnishing.

Serves eight

Now and Later

When your recipe calls for boneless chicken breasts, freeze the skin and bones until you have enough to make chicken broth for soup. To enhance the flavor of your soup or stock, use the bones from roasted turkey or rib roast.

Fruit in Lemon Pear Sauce

Serve this in a clear glass bowl to show off the layers to maximum effect.
It is a great addition to a brunch menu.

1 (29-ounce) can pear halves in heavy syrup
1 egg, beaten
2 tablespoons flour
1 teaspoon butter
2 teaspoons lemon juice
1 pint strawberries, sliced
1 cup whipping cream
2 tablespoons confectioners' sugar
1 (16-ounce) can pineapple chunks, drained
2 medium bananas, sliced
1 (11-ounce) can mandarin oranges, drained
2 or 3 kiwifruit, chilled, peeled, sliced
1/4 cup slivered almonds, toasted

Drain the pears, reserving 1 cup syrup. Cut 4 pear halves into halves lengthwise and reserve for topping. Chop the remaining pears.

Combine the reserved pear syrup, egg and flour in a medium saucepan and mix well. Cook over medium heat until thickened, stirring constantly. Stir in the butter and lemon juice. Cool to room temperature.

Whip the cream with the confectioners' sugar in a mixing bowl until soft pcaks form. Fold into the cooled mixture.

Reserve several strawberry slices to top the dish. Layer the chopped pears, pineapple, bananas, strawberries and oranges in a large glass bowl. Spread the cooked mixture over the top. Chill, covered, for 8 hours or longer.

Arrange the kiwifruit, reserved strawberries and reserved pears over the top just before serving. Sprinkle with the almonds.

Serves eight to ten

Artichoke Salad with Lima Beans and Peas

Usher in spring with this unusual salad.

Creamy Vinaigrette
> 2 tablespoons heavy cream
> 1/4 cup red wine vinegar
> 2 tablespoons minced shallots
> 1/4 cup extra-virgin olive oil
> salt and pepper to taste

Salad
> 2 (14-ounce) cans chicken broth
> 1 (16-ounce) package frozen baby lima beans
> 2 (14-ounce) cans water-pack artichoke hearts, drained,
>   cut into quarters
> 1 (16-ounce) package frozen tiny peas
> 1/4 cup chopped fresh mint
> salt and pepper to taste

Garnish
> fresh mint sprigs
> 1/4 cup chopped pimentos or roasted red pepper

For the vinaigrette, combine the cream, vinegar and shallots in a small bowl and whisk to mix well. Add the olive oil gradually, whisking constantly. Season with salt and pepper.

For the salad, bring the chicken broth to a simmer in a large saucepan. Add the lima beans. Simmer, covered, for 10 minutes or until tender. Remove to a large bowl with a slotted spoon.

Add the artichoke hearts to the broth in the saucepan. Cook for 2 minutes. Add the peas. Cook, covered, for 3 minutes or until heated through. Remove to the bowl with the beans with a slotted spoon.

Add the chopped mint and the desired amount of the vinaigrette to the vegetables and toss to coat well. Season with salt and pepper. Serve warm or at room temperature.

Garnish with mint sprigs and pimentos or roasted red pepper.

Serves ten

Mayonnaise Magic

To add kick to ordinary mayonnaise, mix the following ingredients with 1 cup of mayonnaise:

*For **Aïoli Mayonnaise**, add 4 crushed garlic cloves and 1/2 teaspoon coarse salt. Serve with crudités or cold fish.*

*For **Andalusian Mayonnaise**, add 2 crushed garlic cloves and 2 tablespoons minced red and green bell pepper. Serve with grilled fish or beef.*

*For **Chantilly Mayonnaise**, fold in 1/4 cup whipped cream. Serve with cold vegetables or poached fish.*

*For **Herbed Mayonnaise**, add 1/2 to 1 cup finely chopped fresh herbs. Serve with barbecued poultry or beef.*

*For **Sun-Dried Tomato Mayonnaise**, add 12 drained and minced oil-pack sun-dried tomatoes. Serve with crudités or grilled chicken or beef.*

*For **Lemon Mayonnaise**, add 2 teaspoons grated lemon zest and 1/4 cup fresh lemon juice. Serve with fish or seafood.*

*For **Mediterranean Mayonnaise**, add 1/4 cup chopped fresh parsley, 1/4 cup minced green onions, 2 tablespoons chopped capers and 1 teaspoon hot sauce. Serve with grain salads, crudités, or grilled meats.*

*For **Roasted Red Pepper Mayonnaise**, add 1/2 cup chopped roasted red pepper.*

Blue Ridge Black Bean Salad

Colorful, nutritious, and low in fat—the very foundation of the food pyramid.

Lime Vinaigrette
2 tablespoons fresh lime juice
2 tablespoons balsamic vinegar
2 tablespoons olive oil
2 teaspoons ground cumin
red pepper flakes to taste
salt and black pepper to taste

Salad
2 or 3 (16-ounce) cans black beans, drained, rinsed
1 (11-ounce) can white Shoe Peg corn, drained
1 to 2 cups cooked brown rice
2 (14-ounce) cans diced tomatoes
1 each green, red and yellow bell pepper, chopped
1 purple onion, chopped
1/2 cup chopped fresh cilantro

For the vinaigrette, combine the lime juice, vinegar, olive oil, cumin and red pepper flakes in a bowl and whisk to mix well. Whisk in salt and black pepper to taste.

For the salad, combine the beans, corn, rice, undrained tomatoes, bell peppers, onion and cilantro in a large bowl and mix well. Add the vinaigrette and toss to mix. Chill, covered, in the refrigerator for up to several days.

Serves ten to twelve

Bibb Salad with Raspberry Maple Dressing

This can also be tossed together for entertaining, but it needs to be served immediately as it will wilt quickly.

Raspberry Maple Dressing
2/3 cup vegetable oil
1/4 cup raspberry vinegar
2 tablespoons real maple syrup

Salad
5 heads Bibb lettuce, torn
2 small purple onions, thinly sliced into rings
2 cups crumbled feta or bleu cheese
1/2 cup pine nuts, toasted

For the dressing, combine the oil, raspberry vinegar and maple syrup in a covered jar with a lid. Cover and shake to mix well.

For the salad, arrange the lettuce on serving plates and arrange the onion rings over the top. Sprinkle with the cheese and pine nuts. Drizzle with the dressing.

Serves twelve

Chopped Salad with Bleu Cheese and Avocado

The secret to this salad is to chop the vegetables into pieces uniform in size.

Basic Vinaigrette
3/4 cup vegetable oil
1/4 cup vinegar
1 garlic clove, minced
4 teaspoons sugar
1 teaspoon salt
pepper to taste

Salad
1 large head romaine lettuce, finely chopped or shredded
1 large tomato, chopped
1 medium red onion, chopped
1 large avocado, chopped
3 ounces bleu cheese, crumbled
6 slices bacon, crisp-fried, crumbled

For the vinaigrette, combine the oil, vinegar, garlic, sugar, salt and pepper in a jar with a lid. Cover and shake to mix well.

For the salad, place the lettuce in an oval or rectangular bowl. Arrange the tomato, onion, avocado, cheese and bacon in rows over the lettuce. Drizzle with the vinaigrette and toss just before serving.

Serves six

Cooking Bacon

Arrange thick slices of center-cut bacon on a baking sheet covered with foil. Bake at 350 degrees for 6 minutes. Turn the bacon and bake for 2 to 3 minutes longer or until crisp. This makes for easy cleanup, eliminates spatters, and the bacon will turn out flat and perfect every time.

Avocados

The most common varieties of avocado are the Haas, which has a dark and bumpy skin, and the larger Fuerte, which has a smooth and thinner skin. Avocados should be used as soon as possible as they discolor quickly, but they should never be chilled, as it will cause them to turn black. Placing the avocado pit in the prepared dish until serving time will reduce the amount of discoloration, as will covering the dish with lemon slices, lime slices, or plastic wrap placed directly on the surface. To keep chopped or sliced avocados green for salads before tossing, float them in a mixture of water and lemon juice; drain to serve.

Green Salad Extraordinaire with Poppy Seed Dressing

The citrus fruit in this salad gives it a lightness that makes it the perfect accompaniment to a substantial entrée.

Poppy Seed Dressing
1 cup vegetable oil
$1/2$ cup tarragon vinegar
$1/2$ cup sugar
1 tablespoon poppy seeds
1 teaspoon grated onion
1 teaspoon dry mustard
$3/4$ teaspoon onion salt
1 teaspoon salt

Salad
16 ounces mixed lettuces
16 ounces small spinach leaves
2 medium avocados, sliced
1 pint strawberries, cut into halves
1 to 2 cantaloupes, cut into balls
1 pint cherry tomatoes, cut into halves
2 cucumbers, peeled, sliced
8 ounces fresh mushrooms, sliced

For the dressing, combine the oil, vinegar, sugar, poppy seeds, onion, dry mustard, onion salt and salt in a jar with a lid. Cover and shake to mix well. Store in the refrigerator until needed.

For the salad, tear the lettuces and spinach into a large salad bowl. Add the avocados, strawberries, cantaloupe balls, tomatoes, cucumbers and mushrooms. Add the dressing at serving time and toss to mix well.

Serves eighteen

Mixed Greens with Pears and Pear Vinaigrette

Pear Vinaigrette
$^1/_2$ cup chopped peeled fresh pear
$^1/_4$ cup rice vinegar
1 teaspoon (scant) sesame oil
2 tablespoons orange juice
3 tablespoons olive oil
salt and freshly ground pepper to taste

Salad
$^1/_2$ red onion, thinly sliced into rings
1 tablespoon sesame seeds
10 to 12 ounces mixed baby
    salad greens
2 pears, thinly sliced
2 avocados, thinly sliced

For the vinaigrette, combine the pear and vinegar in a food processor container and process until smooth. Add the sesame oil and orange juice and process until well mixed. Add the olive oil gradually, processing constantly until combined. Season with salt and pepper. Store in the refrigerator for up to 2 days.

For the salad, combine the onion with 2 tablespoons of the vinaigrette in a bowl. Let stand at room temperature for 30 minutes or in the refrigerator for up to 6 hours. Sprinkle the sesame seeds on a baking sheet and toast at 350 degrees for 8 to 10 minutes or until golden brown.

Combine the lettuce with the onion and remaining vinaigrette in a bowl and toss to coat well. Spoon onto serving plates and arrange the pear and avocado slices in a spoke design over the top. Sprinkle with the sesame seeds.

Serves six

Mixed Greens with Pink Grapefruit

Raspberry Citrus Vinaigrette
1 tablespoon orange juice
2 tablespoons raspberry vinegar
1 tablespoon balsamic vinegar
2 teaspoons extra-virgin olive oil
$^1/_2$ teaspoon reduced-sodium soy sauce
$^1/_4$ teaspoon Dijon mustard
$^1/_2$ teaspoon sugar
$^1/_8$ teaspoon salt
$^1/_4$ teaspoon pepper

Salad
8 cups mixed salad greens
1 cup pink grapefruit sections
1 cup thinly sliced red onion
$^1/_4$ cup chopped walnuts

For the vinaigrette, combine the orange juice, raspberry vinegar, balsamic vinegar, olive oil, soy sauce, Dijon mustard, sugar, salt and pepper in a small bowl and mix well.

For the salad, combine the salad greens, grapefruit, onion and walnuts in a large bowl. Drizzle with the vinaigrette and toss to coat well.

Serves six

Homemade Croutons

Freshly made croutons are easy to make and much better than stale bread in a box. Melt 3 tablespoons unsalted butter with 3 tablespoons olive oil in a large skillet over medium heat and add 4 cups of 1/2-inch dried bread cubes, tossing to coat well. Reduce the heat to low and sauté for 15 to 20 minutes or until light golden brown. Add 1 minced garlic clove, 1/2 cup mixed fresh herbs or 2 teaspoons dried herbs and season with salt and pepper to taste. Sauté for 5 minutes longer. Combine with 1/2 cup grated Parmesan cheese in a bowl and toss to mix well. Cool to room temperature and store in an airtight bag in the refrigerator. You may recrisp the croutons on a baking sheet in a 275-degree oven if necessary.

Potato and Spinach Salad with Bacon Vinaigrette

1 pound Yukon Gold potatoes, peeled
1 red bell pepper, roasted (see page 25)
1 slice bacon, chopped
3 tablespoons red wine vinegar
2 tablespoons extra-virgin olive oil
1 garlic clove, minced
2 1/2 ounces small spinach leaves
1 cup thinly sliced celery
salt and pepper to taste

Cut the potatoes into 3/4-inch pieces. Cook in water in a saucepan for 7 minutes or until tender; drain. Combine with the chopped bell pepper in a bowl and mix gently.

Fry the bacon in a skillet for 3 minutes or until crisp; drain. Whisk the vinegar, olive oil and garlic in a small saucepan. Cook over low heat for 1 minute or just until heated through, stirring constantly. Stir in the bacon. Add to the potato and bell pepper mixture.

Add the spinach and celery and toss to mix well. Season with salt and pepper and serve immediately.

Serves four

Roasted New Potato Salad

4 cups quartered unpeeled new potatoes
1/2 cup mayonnaise
1/2 cup sour cream
1/4 cup chopped green onions
1/4 teaspoon salt
pepper to taste
8 slices bacon, crisp-fried, crumbled

Spread the potatoes in a roasting pan sprayed with nonstick cooking spray. Roast at 425 degrees for 40 minutes or until tender and golden brown. Cool slightly.

Combine the mayonnaise, sour cream, green onions, salt and pepper in a large bowl and mix well. Add the potatoes and bacon and toss gently to mix. Serve warm or at room temperature.

Serves six

The Greenbrier's Radicchio and Mixed Greens with Apples and Blue Cheese

Apple Vinaigrette
2 tablespoons apple juice
2 tablespoons sherry vinegar
1 garlic clove, crushed
$1/3$ cup canola oil
salt and pepper to taste

Salad
4 cups mixed salad greens
$1/3$ cup crumbled blue cheese
$1/4$ head radicchio, julienned
4 outer radicchio leaves
1 red apple, cut into $1/8$-inch slices
$1/4$ cup sliced green onions

For the vinaigrette, whisk the apple juice, vinegar and garlic in a small bowl. Whisk in the oil gradually. Season with salt and pepper.

For the salad, combine the salad greens with the vinaigrette, $1/4$ cup of the cheese and the juilienned radicchio in a bowl and toss to coat well. Spoon onto the radicchio leaves on serving plates.

Fan the apple slices over the salad and sprinkle with the remaining cheese and green onions. Serve immediately.

Serves four

Caesar Salad

Top with strips of grilled or blackened chicken for a main-dish salad.

1 large garlic clove, minced
2 tablespoons fresh lemon juice
1 tablespoon Worcestershire sauce
1 teaspoon Dijon mustard
3 tablespoons sour cream
$1/4$ teaspoon pepper
$1/2$ cup olive oil
2 heads Romaine lettuce, torn into bite-sized pieces
$1/3$ cup grated Parmesan cheese
Homemade Croutons (page 52)

Combine the garlic, lemon juice, Worcestershire sauce, Dijon mustard, sour cream and pepper in a bowl and mix well. Add the olive oil gradually, stirring constantly to mix well. Chill, covered, until serving time. Combine the dressing with the lettuce and cheese in a salad bowl and toss to mix well. Top with Homemade Croutons.

Serves eight

Fresh From the Freezer

For freshness of flavor, nothing compares to homemade stock. Make the stock in quantity and freeze it in ice cube trays. You can also freeze gravy, milk, or cream in ice cubes trays. Remove the cubes from the trays when firm and store in plastic bags in the freezer, ready in any amount needed.

Sweet-and-Sour Slaw

A sweet-and-sour accent to favorite southern foods. Try it with fried chicken or barbecued pork.

1 cup sugar
1 (2-pound) head cabbage
3/4 cup finely chopped onion
1 cup white wine vinegar
3/4 cup canola, safflower or soy oil
1 tablespoon dry mustard
1 tablespoon celery seeds
1 teaspoon salt

Reserve 2 tablespoons of the sugar. Discard the outer leaves and core of the cabbage and cut into thin slices. Layer the cabbage and onion in a large bowl until all the ingredients are used, ending with onion and sprinkling each layer with the remaining sugar.

Combine the reserved sugar with the vinegar, oil, dry mustard, celery seeds and salt in a saucepan. Bring to a boil, stirring to mix well. Pour over the layers.

Cover and chill for 24 hours or longer, tossing once or twice to mix well. Toss at serving time and serve cold or at room temperature.

Serves eight

Summertime Tomatoes

6 large Roma tomatoes
6 (8-ounce) balls mozzarella cheese packed in water, drained
1/4 cup red wine vinegar
2 teaspoons Dijon mustard
1/3 cup olive oil
leaves of 1 large bunch basil, torn
2 tablespoons thinly sliced chives
salt and freshly ground pepper to taste

Slice the tomatoes and cheese 1/4 inch thick and arrange alternately in overlapping circles on a large platter.

Combine the vinegar and Dijon mustard in a bowl and whisk until smooth. Whisk in the olive oil. Pour over the tomatoes and cheese. Sprinkle with the basil, chives, salt and pepper.

Serves twelve

Stacked Grits and Spinach Salad

An inventive salad with a great presentation.

Grits
1 (14-ounce) can chicken broth
1 cup quick-cooking grits
1 1/2 cups shredded Cheddar cheese
2 tablespoons butter or margarine

Salad
1/2 cup broken pecans (optional)
7 cups shredded fresh spinach
4 slices bacon, crisp-fried, crumbled
1/2 cup shredded Cheddar cheese
1 (8-ounce) bottle Italian salad dressing

For the grits, bring the chicken broth to a boil in a saucepan. Stir in the grits gradually. Cook for 4 to 5 minutes or until thick, stirring frequently. Add the cheese and stir until the cheese melts.

Pour into a lightly greased 9×9-inch dish. Chill, covered, in the refrigerator. Cut into 4 squares and cut the squares diagonally to make 8 triangles. Split each triangle horizontally to make 16 triangles. Sauté in the butter in a large skillet for 2 minutes on each side or until light brown. Remove to serving plates, reserving the drippings.

For the salad, sauté the pecans in the drippings in the skillet for 2 minutes or until golden brown; drain. Combine with the spinach, bacon, cheese and salad dressing in a bowl and toss to mix well. Stack the grits and salad on serving plates.

Serves four

Sweet Onion and Tomato Salad with Corn and Basil

Basil Vinaigrette
1 tablespoon chopped fresh basil
2 tablespoons white balsamic vinegar
2 teaspoons extra-virgin olive oil
1 teaspoon Dijon mustard

Salad
1/2 cup fresh basil leaves
2 large tomatoes, thinly sliced
1/2 cup thinly sliced Vidalia onion or other sweet onion
1 cup fresh white corn kernels

For the vinaigrette, combine the basil, vinegar, olive oil and Dijon mustard in a bowl and mix well.

For the salad, combine the basil leaves, tomatoes, onion and corn in a bowl. Add the vinaigrette and toss lightly to mix.

Serves four

Minted Couscous Salad

3/4 cup water
1/2 cup uncooked couscous
salt to taste
3 tablespoons each olive oil and safflower oil
3 tablespoons fresh lemon juice
pepper to taste
1/4 cup slivered almonds, lightly toasted
1/4 cup chopped tomato
1/4 cup finely chopped red onion
1/4 cup crumbled feta cheese
2 tablespoons chopped fresh mint leaves

Bring the water to a boil in a saucepan. Stir in the couscous and salt. Remove from the heat and cover; let stand for 5 minutes.

Combine the olive oil, safflower oil, lemon juice, salt and pepper in a bowl and mix well. Add the couscous and mix well. Let stand at room temperature for 2 hours. Add the almonds, tomato, onion, cheese and mint and toss lightly.

Serves four as a salad or two as a main dish

The Greenbrier's Wild Rice Salad

1 cup uncooked wild rice
6 cups water
2 large oranges
1/4 cup dried cherries
2 scallions, finely chopped
1/2 cup finely chopped flat-leaf parsley
1 1/2 tablespoons olive oil
1 1/2 tablespoons balsamic vinegar, or to taste
1 1/2 tablespoons fresh orange juice, or to taste
hot sauce to taste
salt and freshly ground pepper to taste

Garnish
sprigs of flat-leaf parsley

Rinse the wild rice in cold water in a strainer. Combine with water to cover in a large bowl and let stand for 4 hours; drain.

Combine the rice with 6 cups water in a large saucepan. Bring to a boil and reduce the heat. Simmer for 30 minutes or until tender.

Cut the peel from the oranges and remove the sections with a knife, catching the juice in a bowl; set the orange sections aside. Add the dried cherries to the orange juice in the bowl and let stand for 5 minutes or longer.

Reserve several orange sections for topping the salad and combine the remaining orange sections with the rice, dried cherries, scallions and parsley in a bowl; mix well. Add the olive oil, vinegar, 1 1/2 tablespoons orange juice, hot sauce, salt and pepper and toss to mix well. Top with the reserved orange sections and garnish with parsley leaves.

Serves six

Mediterranean Pasta Salad

Garlic Vinaigrette
1 tablespoon minced garlic
1/4 cup red wine vinegar
1/4 cup fresh lemon juice
2 teaspoons sugar
1/4 cup olive oil

Salad
1/4 cup pine nuts
4 cups cooked tri-color rotini, chilled
1/2 cup chopped red bell pepper
1/2 cup thinly sliced scallions
1/2 cup thinly sliced black olives
1/2 cup finely chopped sun-dried tomatoes
1 cup crumbled feta cheese
1 tablespoon salt
1 teaspoon freshly ground pepper

For the vinaigrette, combine the garlic, vinegar, lemon juice and sugar in a small bowl. Add the olive oil gradually, whisking constantly to mix well.

For the salad, spread the pine nuts on a baking sheet and roast at 350 degrees for 10 minutes, checking frequently to prevent overbrowning. Combine with the pasta, bell pepper, scallions, black olives, sun-dried tomatoes and cheese in a large bowl and toss to mix well. Toss with the vinaigrette and season with the salt and pepper.

Serves four

The Art Museum and ArtVenture

The Art Museum of Western Virginia, a Center in the Square tenant, is nationally recognized as an exhibitor of important works of art from cultures around the world, with a special emphasis on American art, the Hudson Valley School, and artistic expressions of the Blue Ridge.

The Art Museum encourages extraordinary enthusiasm for the visual arts. Visitors discover stunning exhibits and creative programs. Tours, gallery talks, family days, classes, and camps are part of the Art Museum's regular programming.

In 1991, the Art Museum and the League entered into a unique partnership geared to the children of the Roanoke Valley. ArtVenture is an interactive learning center offering an exciting hands-on approach to experiencing art. Sculpture puzzles and a Plexiglas painting screen, among other exhibits, allow children to explore their own creativity. ArtVenture's unique presentation nurtures both children and the art within those children.

★ *Sidebar Stars*
Kelly and Russ Ellis

Orzo Salad with Turkey and Black Beans

This piquant salad works well as a main dish.

Piquant Salad Dressing
2 garlic cloves, minced
1/2 teaspoon salt
3 tablespoons fresh lime juice
1 1/2 tablespoons white wine vinegar
1 or 2 jalapeño peppers, seeded, chopped, or Tabasco sauce to taste
1 1/2 teaspoons ground cumin, or to taste
salt and pepper to taste
2/3 cup olive oil

Salad
8 ounces uncooked orzo
salt to taste
4 cups chopped cooked turkey
2 (15-ounce) cans black beans, rinsed, drained
1 red bell pepper, finely chopped
1 yellow bell pepper, finely chopped
1 red onion, cut into quarters lengthwise, thinly sliced crosswise
1/3 cup finely chopped fresh cilantro
shredded romaine lettuce
2 avocados, chopped

For the salad dressing, mash the garlic with 1/2 teaspoon salt in a small bowl. Combine with the lime juice, vinegar, jalapeño peppers, cumin and salt and pepper to taste in a blender or food processor container; process until smooth. Add the olive oil gradually, processing constantly until well mixed.

For the salad, cook the pasta al dente in a large saucepan of salted water; drain in a colander and rinse under cold water. Cool to room temperature.

Combine the pasta with the turkey, beans, bell peppers, onion and cilantro in a large bowl. Add the salad dressing and toss to mix well. Spoon onto a platter lined with romaine lettuce and top with the avocados.

Serves ten to twelve

Chilled Chicken and Pasta Salad

Onion Dressing

1^1/2 tablespoons grated onion
3 tablespoons red wine vinegar
3 tablespoons lemon juice
1^1/2 tablespoons sugar
1^1/2 teaspoons dried basil, crushed
1^1/2 teaspoons seasoned salt
^{1}/3 cup olive oil

Salad

4 to 6 chicken breasts
^{1}/4 cup chopped onion
2^1/2 cups chicken broth
6 ounces uncooked vermicelli
1 (14-ounce) can artichoke hearts, drained, cut into
    quarters
1 pint cherry tomatoes, cut into halves

For the dressing, combine the onion, vinegar, lemon juice, sugar, basil and seasoned salt in a bowl. Add the olive oil gradually, whisking to mix well. Chill, covered, in the refrigerator.

For the salad, simmer the chicken with the onion in the chicken broth in a saucepan for 45 minutes or until tender. Remove the chicken from the broth; strain and reserve the broth. Cool the chicken and chop coarsely.

Break the pasta into 2-inch pieces. Bring the reserved broth to a boil in the saucepan and add the pasta. Cook until tender; drain.

Combine the chicken and pasta with the salad dressing in a bowl and mix gently. Add the artichoke hearts and toss to coat well. Chill, covered, in the refrigerator for 2 hours or longer. Add the cherry tomatoes at serving time and toss gently.

Serves six to eight

Variety Vinaigrettes

For **Basic Vinaigrette,** process ^{1}/3 cup vinegar with 1 teaspoon sugar, ^{1}/2 teaspoon salt and ^{1}/2 teaspoon freshly ground pepper in a food processor. Add ^{2}/3 cup extra-virgin olive oil in a steady stream, processing constantly. Let stand at room temperature for up to 10 hours.

For **Parmesan Vinaigrette,** stir in 3 tablespoons freshly grated Parmesan cheese.

For **Roquefort Vinaigrette,** add 1 to 2 tablespoons crumbled Roquefort cheese.

For **Herbed Vinaigrette,** add 1 tablespoon fines herbes.

For **Mustard Vinaigrette,** use balsamic vinegar and add 1 tablespoon Dijon mustard and 2 minced garlic cloves.

For **Curry Vinaigrette,** add 1 tablespoon lightly sautéed curry powder. Serve over stronger-flavored greens such as chicory, escarole or spinach.

For **Shallot Vinaigrette,** use 2 tablespoons vinegar and process with 1 egg yolk, 1 tablespoon Dijon mustard and 1 shallot. Use ^{3}/4 cup olive oil.

For **Tarragon Vinaigrette,** mix equal parts sherry wine vinegar and lemon juice with 2 parts each of olive oil and safflower oil. Add 1 tablespoon each fresh tarragon and chervil.

Cafe Succotash's Sesame Ginger Salad Dressing

Combine 1/3 cup rice wine vinegar, 2 tablespoons soy sauce, 2 teaspoons dry mustard, 4 teaspoons sugar and 2 teaspoons grated gingerroot in a blender or food processor container and process until smooth, scraping the container once or twice. Mix 1 cup peanut oil or other vegetable oil with 2 tablespoons sesame oil in a bowl. Add to the blender very gradually, processing constantly until smooth. Chill, covered, for 1 hour or longer to blend the flavors. Shake at serving time. Serve on your favorite garden salad, spinach salad or pasta salad.

Chicken Salad Fit for the Queen

Queen Elizabeth was served this curried chicken salad on a visit to the University of Virginia in Charlottesville in 1976.

Curry Salad Dressing
3/4 cup mayonnaise
2 teaspoons lemon juice
2 teaspoons soy sauce
1 teaspoon curry powder

Salad
2 cups (1/2-inch) cooked chicken cubes
1/4 cup sliced water chestnuts
8 ounces seedless green grapes, cut into halves
1 (8-ounce) can pineapple chunks, drained
1/2 cup chopped celery
1/2 cup toasted slivered almonds

For the salad dressing, combine the mayonnaise, lemon juice, soy sauce and curry powder in a bowl and mix well.

For the salad, combine the chicken, water chestnuts, grapes, pineapple, celery and almonds in a large bowl. Add the salad dressing and toss to mix well. Chill for several hours.

Serves six

Hotel Roanoke's Grilled Halibut Salad

Perfect for a light and lovely luncheon.

Artichoke Vinaigrette
1 (14-ounce) can artichoke hearts, drained
1/4 cup red wine vinegar
1 teaspoon honey
1 tablespoon Dijon mustard
1/4 cup chicken stock
salt and pepper to taste
1/2 cup olive oil

Salad
12 to 14 ounces fresh halibut fillets
chopped garlic to taste
Old Bay seasoning, salt and pepper to taste
12 fresh asparagus spears
4 to 6 cups mixed tender salad greens, such as mâche, red leaf lettuce,
    Boston lettuce or Bibb lettuce
4 Roma tomatoes, cut into quarters

For the vinaigrette, purée the artichoke hearts in a blender or food processor. Add the vinegar, honey, Dijon mustard, chicken stock, salt and pepper and process until smooth. Add the olive oil gradually, processing until well mixed.

For the salad, sprinkle the halibut with garlic, Old Bay seasoning, salt and pepper. Grill until cooked through. Chill, covered, in the refrigerator.

Cut the asparagus into 4-inch pieces. Combine with 3/4 cup of the vinaigrette in a shallow dish. Marinate, covered, in the refrigerator for 2 to 3 hours.

Divide the salad greens between the serving plates. Break up the halibut and arrange around the lettuce. Arrange the asparagus tent-fashion with the tips up. Arrange the tomato quarters around the plate and drizzle with the remaining vinaigrette. Serve with toast points or cracker bread.

Serves four

A Cut Above

Meats & Poultry

Virginia is for Winers

Thomas Jefferson once wrote, "Good wine is a necessity of life for me." For the many others who believe in the tonic power of the grape, Virginia is a destination spot.

In 1992, Wine Spectator declared Virginia "America's most promising emerging wine region." Now more than fifty wineries dot the map, and Virginia is the nation's sixth-largest producer of fine wine.

In addition to promising wines, Virginia's wineries promise good fun. Dozens of wine festivals attract thousands of visitors annually. Located close to home at Milepost 171.5 off the Parkway, Chateau Morrissette is home to award-winning wine, a first-class restaurant, and the very popular Black Dog Jazz Concert Series.

Other wineries routinely offer tours, tastings, special dinners, and the ritual blessing of the harvest. If good wine is the necessity, and fun an ancillary benefit, then the festivities, superb harvests, and the wine-making techniques of Virginia's vintners would make Mr. Jefferson proud.

Meats & Poultry

Deluxe Pot Roast

This recipe is from the Southern Living *1990 Annual Recipes.*

1 (4- to 5-pound) boneless chuck roast
2 large garlic cloves, thinly sliced
$^1/_2$ teaspoon salt
$^1/_2$ teaspoon pepper
$^1/_4$ cup flour
$^1/_3$ cup olive oil
1 medium onion, sliced
1 cup burgundy or other dry red wine
1 (8-ounce) can tomato sauce
1 tablespoon brown sugar
1 teaspoon prepared horseradish
1 teaspoon prepared mustard
1 teaspoon dried oregano leaves
1 bay leaf
8 small red potatoes, peeled
6 carrots, scraped, cut into quarters
4 ribs celery, cut into 2-inch pieces

Garnish
fresh oregano sprigs

Cut slits halfway through the long side of the roast. Insert the garlic slices into the slits. Sprinkle with the salt and pepper and shake with the flour in a sealable plastic bag, coating well. Brown on all sides in the olive oil in a heavy saucepan. Add the onion and wine.

Mix the tomato sauce, brown sugar, horseradish, mustard and dried oregano in a bowl. Spoon over the roast and add the bay leaf. Bring to a boil and reduce the heat. Simmer, covered, for 1$^1/_2$ hours. Add the potatoes, carrots and celery. Simmer for 1 hour longer or until the roast and vegetables are tender.

Remove the roast to a serving platter. Arrange the vegetables around the roast. Discard the bay leaf and spoon the pan juices over the top. Garnish with oregano sprigs.
Serves eight to ten

The Texas Tavern

"Roanoke's Millionaires' Club," or the Texas Tavern, serves "1000 people, 10 at a time." As one of the aging signs decorating the walls warns, "We don't cash checks, and we don't play with bumblebees."

Still, since 1930, Roanoke's oldest continuously operating restaurant has lured customers twenty-four hours a day, seven days a week, serving favorites like the Cheesy Western or a Bowl With—a cheeseburger with a fried egg on top or chili with onions, to the uninitiated. And nobody, it seems, remains uninitiated for long. Almost any tour of Roanoke and many a night on the town culminate in a visit.

It began when a carnival man, seeking to cash in on hungry rail travelers, opened the TT, and it has been owned and managed by the same family for four generations. It and Roanoke are now savoring the new chillenium— and the heat goes on.

Bouquet Garni

The classic bouquet garni is a combination of thyme, bay leaves, parsley, and celery, typically tied together with kitchen string or wrapped in cheesecloth. It is placed in a dish as it cooks to gradually release its flavors. For some new twists on the classic favorite, try:

Beef Garni made of pared orange zest, rosemary, thyme, and parsley

Fish and Shellfish Garni made of pared lemon zest, tarragon, and dill

Pork Garni made of sprigs of fresh sage, thyme, and marjoram

Poultry Garni made of a celery rib, a sprig each of parsley, thyme, marjoram, and tarragon, and a bay leaf

Game Garni made of the Poultry Garni with the addition of 6 juniper berries

Vegetable Garni made of bay leaf, savory, sage, marjoram, oregano, and parsley.

Beef Tenderloin with Herb and Garlic Crust

2 tablespoons olive oil	6 garlic cloves, minced
2 (2¹/4- to 2³/4-pound) thick-end portions beef tenderloin, trimmed	2¹/2 tablespoons minced fresh rosemary
	2¹/2 tablespoons minced fresh thyme
salt and pepper to taste	6 tablespoons Dijon mustard
6 tablespoons olive oil	

Rub 1 tablespoon olive oil over each beef tenderloin and sprinkle with salt and pepper. Heat 2 large nonstick skillets over high heat. Add 1 tenderloin to each skillet and cook for 5 minutes or until brown on all sides. Remove to a large roasting pan.

Combine 6 tablespoons olive oil, garlic and 2 tablespoons each of the rosemary and thyme in a small bowl. Coat the top and sides of the beef with the Dijon mustard and herbed oil mixture. Insert a meat thermometer into the thickest portion of 1 tenderloin. Roast at 375 degrees for 45 minutes or to 125 degrees on the meat thermometer for medium-rare. Remove to a platter and let stand for 10 minutes.

Carve the beef into ¹/2-inch slices. Sprinkle with the remaining ¹/2 teaspoon rosemary and thyme. Serve with Red and Yellow Pepper Relish (below).

Serves ten

Red and Yellow Pepper Relish

2 tablespoons butter	¹/3 cup coarsely chopped kalamata olives
2 tablespoons olive oil	
1 large onion, thinly sliced	1 tablespoon Dijon mustard
1 red bell pepper, coarsely chopped	
	1 large garlic clove, chopped
1 yellow bell pepper, coarsely chopped	salt and pepper to taste

Melt the butter with the olive oil in a heavy large skillet over medium-high heat. Add the onion and sauté for 5 minutes or until golden brown. Add the bell peppers and sauté for 3 minutes or just until tender. Add the olives, Dijon mustard and garlic. Cook for 1 minute, stirring constantly. Remove from the heat and season with salt and pepper.

Spoon into a serving bowl. Chill, covered, for 8 hours to 2 days. Return to room temperature to serve.

Makes two cups

Rib Roast with Fresh Thyme and Mustard Jus

1 (3¹/2- to 4-pound) boneless beef rib roast, trimmed
¹/2 cup honey-Dijon mustard
2 teaspoons chopped fresh thyme
¹/4 cup dry white wine
¹/2 cup water
1 teaspoon chopped fresh thyme
salt and pepper to taste

Place the roast in a heavy large roasting pan. Mix the Dijon mustard with
2 teaspoons thyme in a small bowl. Rub over the roast. Let stand, covered, at room
temperature for 1¹/2 hours or in the refrigerator for 8 hours or longer. Scrape the
mustard mixture from the roast and reserve. Insert a meat thermometer into the
thickest portion of the roast.

Roast the beef at 375 degrees for 1 hour. Brush with the reserved mustard
mixture. Roast for 10 minutes longer or to 120 degrees on the meat thermometer.
Remove to a cutting board and tent with foil.

Pour the pan juices into a 1-cup measure and skim off the grease. Place the
roasting pan on the stove top over medium heat and add the degreased pan juices, wine
and water; stir to deglaze the pan. Cook until the mixture is reduced to ¹/2 cup. Stir in
1 teaspoon thyme.

Carve the roast into ¹/2-inch slices. Sprinkle with salt and pepper. Serve with the
reduced pan juices.

Serves six

Valley Favorite Beef Tenderloin

*The flavors in this recipe, which has circulated among Roanoke cooks
for years, are indescribable.*

1 (4- to 6-pound) beef tenderloin
1 tablespoon ground thyme
¹/4 teaspoon dried oregano
1 teaspoon garlic salt
1 tablespoon seasoned salt
1 teaspoon white pepper
1 teaspoon salt
¹/4 cup Worcestershire sauce
1 cup water

Place the beef tenderloin on a large sheet of heavy-duty foil and rub with the
thyme. Mix the oregano, garlic salt, seasoned salt and white pepper in a small bowl.
Rub on the beef. Bring up the edges of the foil and seal. Let stand in the refrigerator
for 12 hours or longer. Let stand at room temperature for 2 hours.

Remove the beef from the foil and place in a roasting pan. Sprinkle with the salt
and pour the Worcestershire sauce and water over the top. Roast at 400 degrees for
35 minutes or until done to taste.

Serves eight to ten

Beef Fillets Topped with Bleu Cheese

4 (4-ounce) beef fillets
2 teaspoons finely chopped fresh thyme
$1/4$ teaspoon salt
$1/4$ teaspoon pepper
1 tablespoon butter
1 tablespoon olive oil

1 cup dry white wine
$1/2$ cup beef consommé
$1/2$ cup half-and-half
8 small asparagus spears
$1 1/2$ ounces bleu cheese, crumbled

Rub the fillets with the thyme, salt and pepper. Melt the butter with the olive oil in a large saucepan. Add the fillets and cook for 1 to 3 minutes on each side or until done to taste. Remove to a broiler pan and keep warm; reserve the drippings in the saucepan.

Add the wine and consommé to the pan drippings, stirring to deglaze the saucepan. Cook over high heat until reduced to $1/2$ cup, stirring frequently. Add the half-and-half. Cook until reduced to $1/2$ cup, stirring constantly; keep warm.

Steam the asparagus in a small amount of water for 8 minutes; drain. Arrange over the fillets and sprinkle with the cheese. Broil 6 inches from the heat source with the oven door ajar for 2 minutes or until the cheese melts. Serve immediately with the sauce.

Serves four

Rib-Eye Steaks with Roasted Red Peppers and Balsamic Vinegar

$1/2$ cup olive oil
1 tablespoon balsamic vinegar
2 teaspoons minced garlic
2 teaspoons dried rosemary
1 teaspoon freshly ground pepper
4 ($3/4$-inch) rib-eye steaks

salt to taste
1 (7-ounce) jar roasted red peppers,
     drained, cut into strips
$1 1/2$ tablespoons balsamic vinegar
1 teaspoon minced garlic

Combine the olive oil, 1 tablespoon vinegar, 2 teaspoons garlic, rosemary and pepper in a shallow dish and whisk to mix well. Add the steaks, turning to coat well. Marinate at room temperature for 1 hour.

Heat a heavy large skillet over high heat. Remove the steaks from the marinade and sprinkle with salt. Add to the skillet and cook for 4 minutes on each side for medium-rare or until done to taste. Remove to serving plates.

Add the roasted red peppers, $1 1/2$ tablespoons vinegar and 1 teaspoon garlic to the skillet. Cook until heated through, stirring to deglaze the skillet. Spoon over the steaks.

Serves four

Flank Steak with Asparagus and Wild Rice Pilaf

16 asparagus spears
1/3 cup reduced-sodium soy sauce
1/4 cup dry sherry
1 garlic clove, minced
1/8 teaspoon ground red pepper
1/2 teaspoon black pepper
1 (1-pound) flank steak
4 cups julienned spinach
2 cups cooked wild rice
1/2 cup finely chopped celery
2/3 cup chopped green onions
2 teaspoons dark sesame oil

Snap off and discard the tough ends of the asparagus. Cook the spears in a small amount of water in a saucepan for 2 minutes or just until tender-crisp. Drain and chill in the refrigerator.

Combine the soy sauce, wine, garlic, red pepper and black pepper in a small bowl and mix well. Reserve 1/3 cup of the mixture. Combine the remaining soy sauce mixture with the asparagus and flank steak in a sealable plastic bag. Marinate in the refrigerator for 1 hour, turning occasionally.

Drain the steak and asparagus, discarding the marinade. Heat a ridged skillet over medium-high heat and add the asparagus and steak. Cook the flank steak for 5 minutes on each side, turning once. Remove to a platter and tent with foil. Let stand for 5 minutes. Carve the flank steak diagonally into thin slices.

Combine the reserved soy sauce mixture with the spinach, wild rice, celery, green onions and sesame oil in a bowl and toss to coat well. Serve with the steak and asparagus.

Serves four

Best Burgers with Caramelized Onions

Slice 4 medium onions and sprinkle with 2 teaspoons sugar. Cook in 2 teaspoons olive oil in a skillet over low heat for 20 to 25 minutes or until medium brown. Stir in 1/4 cup water, 2 teaspoons balsamic vinegar and 1/4 teaspoon salt. Cook until heated through and keep warm. Combine 1 pound of extra-lean ground beef with 2 tablespoons tomato paste, 1/4 cup chopped fresh parsley, 1/2 teaspoon salt and 1/4 teaspoon pepper. Mix well and shape into 4 patties. Grill, covered, at 350 to 400 degrees for 5 to 6 minutes on each side or until done to taste. Serve on buns with sliced tomatoes and the caramelized onions.

Center in the Square

Center in the Square is home to a renowned professional theater, the Arts Council of the Blue Ridge, and the museums of art, history, and science. These organizations thrive in a restored 1914 furniture warehouse surrounded by shops, galleries, restaurants, and, of course, the Market. They pay no rent, utilities, marketing, building maintenance, or custodial service fees.

The organizations, in turn, channel their resources into quality programming, exhibits, and productions for the public. People flock to Center for social offerings, as well, including Affair in the Square, Center's glittering black tie gala, which draws thousands of revelers.

Center has received critical acclaim and national and international awards for this innovative concept, including accolades from the International Downtown Association, and citations from the Department of Housing and Urban Development. Center has revitalized a once deteriorating downtown and is the epicenter of a cultural and social renaissance.

★ Sidebar Stars

Sibyl Norment Fishburn
Virginia Thomas Shackelford

Cajun Meat Loaf

This may not be your mother's meat loaf, but it takes comfort food to new heights.

1/2 large onion, chopped
1/2 cup chopped green bell pepper
1/2 teaspoon dried thyme
1/4 teaspoon ground cumin
1 teaspoon salt
3/4 teaspoon cayenne pepper
1/2 teaspoon freshly ground black pepper
2 tablespoons olive oil
1 pound lean ground beef
1 egg, beaten
1/4 cup ketchup
1/2 cup fine dry bread crumbs
1 teaspoon Worcestershire sauce
1/4 cup ketchup

Sauté the onion and bell pepper with the thyme, cumin, salt, cayenne pepper and black pepper in the olive oil in a heavy medium skillet over medium-low heat for 10 minutes or until the vegetables are tender.

Combine the ground beef, egg, 1/4 cup ketchup, bread crumbs and Worcestershire sauce in a bowl and mix well. Add the sautéed vegetables and mix well. Shape into a loaf 5 inches wide and 13/4 inches high and place in a baking pan.

Bake at 375 degrees for 20 minutes. Spread 1/4 cup ketchup over the top and bake for 40 minutes longer.

Serves two to four

Grilled Lamb with Mango Salsa

Tangy tropical salsa marries beautifully with lamb, making for a perfectly sublime patio dinner party.

Mango Salsa
4 medium mangoes, peeled, chopped
$1/4$ cup chopped celery
$1/4$ cup finely chopped green onions
$1/4$ cup chopped yellow or red bell pepper
1 jalapeño pepper, seeded, minced
$1/3$ cup chopped fresh cilantro
$1/4$ cup honey
$1/4$ cup olive oil
2 tablespoons fresh lime juice
$1/4$ teaspoon salt

Lamb
1 teaspoon cumin seeds
1 teaspoon coriander seeds
1 cup olive oil
$1/2$ cup chablis or other dry white wine
$1/4$ cup tequila
2 tablespoons fresh lime juice
2 tablespoons minced garlic
2 tablespoons chopped fresh cilantro
2 jalapeño peppers, seeded, minced
$1/2$ teaspoon salt
$1/2$ teaspoon freshly ground pepper
1 (4- to $4^1/2$-pound) boneless leg of lamb

Garnish
fresh cilantro sprigs

For the salsa, combine the mangoes, celery, green onions, bell pepper, jalapeño pepper and cilantro in a bowl. Whisk the honey, olive oil, lime juice and salt in a small bowl. Add to the mango mixture and mix gently. Chill, covered, for 30 minutes or longer.

For the lamb, toast the cumin seeds in a heavy skillet until light brown, stirring constantly. Remove to a small bowl. Add the coriander seeds to the skillet and toast until light brown, stirring constantly. Add to the cumin seeds.

Crush the seed mixture and add the olive oil. Combine with the wine, tequila, lime juice, garlic, cilantro, jalapeño peppers, salt and pepper in a large shallow dish or heavy-duty sealable bag and mix well. Add the lamb, coating well. Marinate in the refrigerator for 8 hours, turning occasionally.

Remove the lamb from the marinade and insert a meat thermometer into the thickest portion. Place on a grill rack over a grill heated to 350 to 400 degrees. Grill for 40 minutes or to 150 degrees on the meat thermometer for medium-rare, turning once.

Carve the lamb into thin slices and serve with the salsa. Garnish with sprigs of fresh cilantro.

Serves eight

Shenandoah Valley

*Take a drive north of Roanoke
to a valley tucked between
the Blue Ridge and Allegheny
mountain ranges. The
Shenandoah River carved this
150-mile stretch of rich land,
named Daughter of the Stars by
native Americans.*

Hazelnut and Mustard Lamb Chops

*Substitute pork chops or veal chops for the lamb
chops for an equally delicious entrée.*

^{1}/4 cup coarse-grain mustard
^{1}/4 cup Dijon mustard
^{1}/4 cup dry white wine
1 cup hazelnuts, coarsely ground
^{1}/4 cup fresh white bread crumbs
1^1/2 teaspoons minced garlic
2 tablespoons chopped
    fresh parsley
4 (1-inch) center-cut lamb chops
freshly ground pepper to taste
2 tablespoons peanut oil or olive oil
1^1/2 tablespoons butter, melted (optional)

Combine the coarse-grain mustard, Dijon mustard and
wine in a shallow dish and whisk to mix well. Mix the
hazelnuts, bread crumbs, garlic and parsley in a shallow dish.

Sprinkle the lamb chops with pepper. Brown in the
heated oil in a heavy 10- to 12-inch skillet over medium
heat for 5 minutes on each side. Remove from the skillet
with tongs and dip into the mustard mixture. Coat with the
hazelnut mixture, pressing to cover well.

Arrange in a lightly buttered baking pan and drizzle
with the melted butter. Bake at 375 degrees for 20 minutes
or until the crust is golden brown and the lamb chops are
tender but still juicy. Serve on a heated platter.

Serves four

Pork Tenderloin on the Grill

Orange Marmalade Basting Sauce
1/2 cup orange marmalade
1/3 cup Dijon mustard
1 tablespoon Worcestershire sauce
1 tablespoon grated gingerroot
1/4 teaspoon salt
1/4 teaspoon freshly ground pepper

Pork
1 tablespoon chopped fresh sage
2 tablespoons chopped fresh thyme
1/4 teaspoon ground cloves or allspice
3 garlic cloves, minced
salt to taste
1 teaspoon freshly ground pepper
1 to 1 1/2 pounds pork tenderloin
2 tablespoons vegetable oil

For the basting sauce, combine the orange marmalade, Dijon mustard, Worcestershire sauce, gingerroot, salt and pepper in a bowl and mix well.

For the pork, combine the sage, thyme, cloves, garlic, salt and pepper in a small bowl and mix well. Rub the tenderloin with the oil and coat evenly with the herb mixture. Marinate, covered, in the refrigerator for 1 hour or longer.

Oil a rack placed 6 inches above heated coals. Insert a meat thermometer into the thickest portion of the tenderloin. Place the tenderloin on the rack away from the direct heat of the coals. Grill, covered, for 45 to 60 minutes or to 160 degrees on the meat thermometer, basting with the basting sauce every 10 minutes.

Remove to a platter and cover loosely with foil. Let stand for 10 minutes. Carve into slices to serve.

Serves four to six

Pork Tenderloin with Mustard Cream Sauce

1 (1-pound) pork tenderloin
1/3 cup flour
1/2 teaspoon each salt and pepper
3 tablespoons butter or margarine
4 green onions

1/3 cup dry white wine
1 cup heavy cream
1/4 cup Dijon mustard
salt and pepper to taste

Cut the pork tenderloin into 1/2-inch slices. Place between pieces of waxed paper and pound to 1/4-inch thickness with a meat mallet. Mix the flour, 1/2 teaspoon salt and 1/2 teaspoon pepper together and coat the pork medallions with the mixture, shaking off the excess.

Sauté the pork medallions 1/3 at a time in the butter in a skillet for 2 minutes on each side; remove to a warm platter, reserving the drippings.

Slice the green onions, keeping the white and green parts separate. Reserve the green portions. Add the white portions to the drippings in the skillet and sauté for 1 minute or until tender. Stir in the wine and cook for 3 minutes or until reduced to 2 tablespoons. Add the cream and simmer for 5 minutes or until thickened to the desired consistency. Whisk in the Dijon mustard and season with salt and pepper to taste.

Spoon over the pork medallions and sprinkle with the reserved green onion tops. Serve immediately.

Serves four

Goobered-Up Smithfield Hams

Peanuts grow in the south-central section of Virginia and are among the state's most important products. Pigs raised in the town of Smithfield are fed peanuts, which provide a distinctive flavor to the hams that are known worldwide as Smithfield hams.

Pork Chops with Curried Apple and Onion Sauce

The cornerstone of an elegant autumn feast.

4 (8-ounce 1-inch) pork chops
1/2 teaspoon thyme
1/2 teaspoon marjoram
salt and pepper to taste
1 tablespoon olive oil
1 large Granny Smith apple, peeled, chopped
1/2 Vidalia onion, chopped
6 garlic cloves, minced
3/4 cup reduced-sodium chicken broth
1/2 cup dry white wine
1/4 cup heavy cream
2 tablespoons honey mustard
1 teaspoon curry powder
1/2 teaspoon thyme
1/2 teaspoon marjoram

Sprinkle the pork chops with 1/2 teaspoon thyme, 1/2 teaspoon marjoram, salt and pepper. Heat the olive oil in a heavy large skillet over medium-high heat. Add the pork chops and cook for 5 minutes on each side or until cooked through. Remove to a platter and tent with foil to keep warm; reserve the drippings.

Add the apple, onion and garlic to the drippings in the skillet. Sauté over medium-high heat for 2 minutes. Add the chicken broth, wine, cream, mustard, curry powder, 1/2 teaspoon thyme and 1/2 teaspoon marjoram. Cook for 5 minutes or until slightly thickened.

Place the pork chops on serving plates and spoon the sauce over the top. Serve immediately.

Serves four

Pork Chops with a Kick

2 tablespoons butter, softened
1/2 cup chopped Vidalia onion
3 garlic cloves, minced
1/4 cup prepared mustard
2 tablespoons cider vinegar
2 tablespoons light brown sugar
1 teaspoon salt

1/4 teaspoon cayenne pepper
2 tablespoons (about) Worcestershire
    sauce
6 (1 1/2-inch) pork chops
3/4 cup ketchup
1/2 cup chili sauce
1/3 cup water

Combine the butter, onion, garlic, mustard, vinegar, brown sugar, salt and cayenne pepper in a bowl. Add enough Worcestershire sauce to make a paste. Spread over the pork chops. Place in a broiler pan.

Broil close to the heat source for 5 minutes. Mix the ketchup, chili sauce and water in a small bowl. Pour over the pork chops. Bake, covered, at 350 degrees for 1 hour or until the pork chops are tender.

Serves six

Scrumptious Sausage Spaghetti Sauce

8 ounces hot Italian sausage
8 ounces sweet Italian sausage
3 tablespoons (or more) water
2 cups chopped onions
1 1/2 cups finely chopped celery
1 large garlic clove, minced
1 (16-ounce) can Italian plum
    tomatoes, drained
1 (16-ounce) can tomato purée

1 cup red wine
1 tablespoon chopped fresh parsley
1 tablespoon chopped fresh oregano
1 teaspoon sugar
1 bay leaf
1/4 teaspoon ground cumin
2 teaspoons salt
1/4 teaspoon ground red or black pepper

Cook the sausages in the water in a skillet until brown on all sides, adding additional water if needed. Remove the sausages to a cutting board, reserving the drippings. Slice the sausages into bite-size pieces.

Add the onions, celery and garlic to the drippings in the skillet and sauté until tender; remove to a bowl with a slotted spoon.

Combine the tomatoes, tomato purée, wine, parsley, oregano, sugar, bay leaf, cumin, salt and pepper in a large saucepan. Add the sausage and sautéed vegetables. Simmer, covered, for 2 hours.

Cool to room temperature and chill for 24 hours to enhance the flavor. Reheat to serve; remove and discard the bay leaf. Serve over hot spaghetti.

Serves six

Billy's Ritz's Veal Chops with Garlic Mashed Potatoes

The patio at Billy's Ritz lures customers in summer. The elegant and eclectic menu keeps them coming year-round.

4 (16- to 18-ounce) veal chops
1 lemon
20 medium shiitake mushroom caps, sliced
4 garlic cloves, chopped
salt and freshly ground pepper to taste
1/4 cup olive oil
12 to 16 fresh sage leaves

4 ounces Parmigiano-Reggiano cheese, thinly sliced
2 tablespoons olive oil
1/2 cup white wine
1 cup veal stock or beef stock
chopped fresh herbs (optional)
Garlic Mashed Potatoes (below)

Cut a horizontal pocket in each veal chop, cutting from the outer edge to the bone and taking care to leave the ends intact.

Squeeze juice from the lemon over the mushrooms. Sauté the mushrooms and garlic with salt and pepper to taste in 1/4 cup olive oil in a sauté pan. Remove from the heat and stir in the sage and Parmigiano-Reggiano cheese. Stuff into the pockets in the veal chops.

Heat 2 tablespoons olive oil in a sauté pan until nearly smoking. Sprinkle the veal chops with salt and add to the sauté pan. Cook until brown on both sides. Remove to a baking pan, reserving the drippings. Place in a 450-degree oven and bake until cooked through.

Add the wine to the sauté pan, stirring to deglaze the pan. Cook until the wine is nearly evaporated. Add the veal stock. Cook until reduced by 1/2. Season with salt, pepper and herbs of choice.

Spoon the sauce onto the serving plates. Place the veal chops in the sauce. Serve with Garlic Mashed Potatoes and green beans.

Serves four

Garlic Mashed Potatoes

1 1/2 pounds Yukon Gold potatoes or other waxy potatoes
12 garlic cloves
salt to taste

1/2 cup (1 stick) butter, melted
3/4 cup sour cream
white pepper to taste
1 cup (about) milk, warmed

Combine the potatoes with garlic, salt and water to cover in a saucepan. Cook until the potatoes are tender; drain. Mash the potatoes and garlic with a potato masher. Add the butter, sour cream, salt and white pepper and mash until smooth. Add enough milk gradually to make of a smooth consistency, mashing to blend well. Adjust the seasonings.

Serves four

Veal Piccata with Capers and Pine Nuts

2 bacon slices, chopped
6 ounces veal scallops
salt and pepper to taste
flour for coating
2 tablespoons olive oil
1/2 cup white wine
2 tablespoons butter
3 tablespoons toasted pine nuts
1 tablespoon drained capers
2 teaspoons minced fresh sage, or 1/2 teaspoon dried sage

Cook the bacon in a heavy large skillet over medium-high heat until crisp. Remove to paper towels to drain. Drain, but do not wash, the skillet.

Pound the veal very thin between waxed paper. Sprinkle with salt and pepper and coat with flour, shaking off the excess. Heat the olive oil in the skillet over medium-high heat and add the veal. Sauté for 1 minute on each side or just until cooked through. Remove to 2 warm plates and keep warm.

Add the wine to the skillet, stirring to deglaze. Cook until reduced to 3 tablespoons. Whisk in the butter, pine nuts, capers, sage and bacon. Spoon over the veal.

Serves two

Venison with Ginger and Garlic

2 tablespoons grated gingerroot
1 teaspoon chopped garlic
2 cups vegetable oil
1 cup soy sauce
1 tablespoon honey
6 to 8 Virginia whitetail deer steaks

Process the gingerroot, garlic, oil, soy sauce and honey in a blender until smooth. Combine with the venison steaks in a nonreactive bowl, coating well. Marinate, covered, in the refrigerator for 2 to 24 hours.

Remove the steaks from the marinade and insert a meat thermometer into the thickest portion of 1 steak. Grill over medium heat for 4 minutes on each side or to 140 degrees on the meat thermometer; do not overcook. Serve with Peach and Vidalia Onion Chutney (at right).

Serves six to eight

Peach and Vidalia Onion Chutney

Combine 4 quarts chopped peaches, 1 cup chopped Vidalia onion, 1 chopped garlic clove, 1 cup raisins and 1 chopped hot pepper in a saucepan. Add 1 quart vinegar, 1/4 cup mustard seeds, 3 cups packed brown sugar, 2 tablespoons ground ginger and 2 teaspoons salt; mix well. Cook over medium heat until thickened, stirring frequently. Spoon into hot sterilized jars, leaving 1/2 inch headspace; seal immediately with 2-piece lids.

Fresh Herb Substitution

To substitute dried herbs for fresh herbs, use 1/4 teaspoon of a ground herb or 1 teaspoon of dried crumbled herb leaves for every tablespoon of the fresh herb.

Seared Venison Tenderloin with Blackberry and Shallot Sauce

Tenderloins
2 Virginia whitetail deer tenderloins
5 garlic cloves, slivered
2 tablespoons olive oil
sea salt and freshly ground pepper to taste

Blackberry and Shallot Sauce
2 small shallots, chopped
1 teaspoon chopped garlic
1 tablespoon olive oil
1 (10-ounce) jar seedless all-fruit blackberry preserves
1 cup chicken broth
1 tablespoon butter
1 teaspoon honey
salt and freshly ground pepper to taste

For the tenderloins, cut 8 to 10 slits in each tenderloin and insert a garlic sliver into each slit. Rub with the olive oil and season generously with sea salt and pepper; insert a meat thermometer into the thickest portion of 1 tenderloin. Sear in a heated cast-iron skillet over medium heat for 5 to 6 minutes on each side or to 140 degrees on the meat thermometer; do not overcook. Remove to a platter and let stand for several minutes.

For the sauce, sauté the shallots and garlic in the olive oil in a skillet. Add the blackberry preserves and chicken broth. Simmer over medium heat for 10 minutes, stirring frequently. Stir in the butter and honey. Season with salt and pepper.

To serve, carve the tenderloins into slices and place on a serving platter. Spoon the sauce over the slices.

Serves six to eight

Herb-Roasted Chicken with Shallots and Garlic

Chicken prepared in this manner is delicious in chicken salads and casseroles.

1 (5-pound) roasting chicken
juice of 1 lemon
salt and pepper to taste
10 fresh thyme sprigs
6 fresh rosemary sprigs
6 fresh sage sprigs
16 shallots, peeled
6 garlic cloves, unpeeled
1/2 cup dry white wine

Sprinkle the cavity of the chicken with lemon juice, salt and pepper. Add half the thyme, rosemary and sage. Truss the chicken with kitchen twine and place breast side up in a shallow roasting pan.

Roast at 400 degrees for 15 minutes. Arrange the shallots and unpeeled garlic cloves around the chicken. Pour the wine over the shallots and garlic. Reserve a few of the remaining fresh herbs for garnish and sprinkle the remaining herbs into the roasting pan. Roast for 45 minutes longer or until the juices run clear when the thickest portion of the thigh is pierced.

Remove the chicken to a serving platter. Arrange the shallots and garlic around the chicken. Sprinkle with the reserved fresh herbs.

Serves four

Alexander's Pecan Chicken

Alexander's is a favorite special-occasion restaurant. This is a longtime customer favorite that is very easily prepared at home.

3 cups pecans
1 cup fine French bread crumbs
1 teaspoon chopped parsley
1/2 teaspoon salt
1/8 teaspoon cayenne pepper
12 boneless skinless chicken breasts
1/2 cup (1 stick) butter, melted
2 tablespoons vegetable oil

Garnish
fresh herbs

Chop the pecans in a food processor. Mix with the bread crumbs, parsley, salt and cayenne pepper in a shall dish. Brush the chicken with some of the butter and coat with the pecan mixture, pressing to form a crust.

Sauté in the remaining butter and oil in a skillet for 1 minute on each side. Remove to a baking dish. Bake at 350 degrees for 10 minutes or until cooked through. Garnish with herbs and serve immediately.

Serves six

Chicken Rosemary

This is known locally as Fetta's Chicken in tribute to its originator. It is a staple for block parties and beach picnics. Plan ahead when preparing Chicken Rosemary and marinate extra chicken. Freeze it in the marinade, ready to thaw and grill.

1 (16-ounce) bottle Italian salad dressing
$1/2$ cup white wine
$1/4$ cup soy sauce
$1/4$ cup (heaping) brown sugar
2 to 4 teaspoons chopped fresh rosemary
1 teaspoon coarsely ground pepper
8 boneless skinless chicken breasts

Combine the salad dressing with the wine, soy sauce, brown sugar, rosemary and pepper in a sealable plastic bag. Add the chicken, coating well.

Marinate in the refrigerator for 8 to 48 hours, mixing occasionally. Remove from the marinade and grill until done to taste.

Serves eight

Zesty Lemon and Mustard Grilled Chicken

The zesty taste of this chicken makes it a favorite for use in chicken salad. The zesty lemon flavor makes it a summertime favorite.

$1/2$ cup lemon juice
$1/4$ cup Dijon mustard
$1^1/2$ tablespoons finely chopped lemon zest
$1/4$ cup finely chopped fresh herbs or 4 teaspoons dried herbs
$3/4$ teaspoon salt
$1/4$ teaspoon pepper
8 boneless skinless chicken breasts

Combine the lemon juice, Dijon mustard, lemon zest, herbs, salt and pepper in a shallow dish and mix well. Add the chicken, coating well. Marinate, covered, in the refrigerator for 2 to 4 hours.

Remove the chicken from the marinade and place on a grill rack 3 inches from the heat source. Grill over medium heat for 8 to 10 minutes on each side or until cooked through.

For the herbs, you may use thyme, rosemary, basil, oregano and/or parsley.

Serves eight

Chicken Quiche with Cheddar and Pecan Crust

A lively way to dress up chicken and even better topped with a dollop of salsa.

Cheddar and Pecan Crust and Topping
1 cup pecan halves
1 cup flour
1 cup shredded sharp Cheddar cheese
1/4 teaspoon paprika
1/2 teaspoon salt
1/3 cup vegetable oil

Quiche Filling
3 eggs, beaten
1/2 cup chicken broth
1 cup sour cream
1/4 cup mayonnaise
2 cups chopped cooked chicken
1/4 cup minced Vidalia onion
1/2 cup shredded sharp Cheddar cheese
4 drops of Tabasco sauce
1/4 teaspoon dried dillweed

Garnish
1 jar medium salsa

For the crust and topping, chop 3/4 cup of the pecans, reserving the remaining pecan halves for the topping. Mix the chopped pecans with the flour, cheese, paprika and salt in a bowl and mix well. Stir in the oil. Reserve 1/4 of the mixture for the topping. Press the remaining mixture over the bottom and up the side of a 9-inch quiche pan; prick the bottom with a fork. Bake at 350 degrees for 10 minutes. Cool to room temperature.

For the filling, combine the eggs, chicken broth, sour cream and mayonnaise in a mixing bowl and mix well. Add the chicken, onion, cheese, Tabasco sauce and dillweed and mix gently. Spoon into the baked crust.

Sprinkle with the reserved pecans and crumb mixture. Bake at 350 degrees for 45 minutes or until set. Garnish with salsa.

Serves six

Packing Popcorn

Gifts by mail are always welcome, but Styrofoam packing peanuts are messy and an environmental nightmare. Consider using ordinary air-popped popcorn as the packing medium for your next fragile gift—a biodegradable alternative recommended by the postal service.

The Greenbrier's Chicken Saltimbocca

4 (4-ounce) boneless skinless chicken breasts
4 (1/2-ounce) thin prosciutto slices
4 (1/2-ounce) slices provolone cheese, Havarti cheese or fontina cheese
2 teaspoons minced fresh sage
1/2 cup flour
salt and pepper to taste
2 teaspoons olive oil
1 garlic clove, crushed
1/3 cup white wine
1 cup chicken stock
1/2 teaspoon cornstarch
1 tablespoon cold water

Garnish
fresh sage

Place the chicken breasts on a work surface and pound lightly. Layer 1 slice of prosciutto and 1 slice of cheese on 1 side of each piece of chicken; sprinkle with the sage. Fold the other side over to enclose the filling. Mix the flour with salt and pepper. Coat both sides of the chicken lightly with the flour mixture.

Heat a large nonstick sauté pan over medium heat. Add the olive oil and heat. Add the garlic and sauté just until the garlic begins to brown. Remove and discard the garlic. Increase the heat to medium-high.

Add the chicken to the sauté pan and sauté until brown on both sides. Add the wine and chicken stock. Reduce the heat and simmer for 3 minutes; do not boil. Remove the chicken to a heated platter and tent with foil to keep warm.

Blend the cornstarch with the cold water in a small bowl. Scrape up the browned bits from the bottom of the skillet with a wooden spoon. Add the cornstarch mixture. Cook until thickened, stirring constantly. Spoon over the chicken. Garnish with fresh sage and serve immediately.

Serves four

Spicy Chicken with Black Bean Purée

Chicken
2 boneless skinless chicken breasts
2 teaspoons fajita seasoning
1 teaspoon olive oil

Black Bean Purée
1 (15-ounce) can black beans
1/2 cup chopped onion
2 garlic cloves, minced
1 (10-ounce) can tomatoes with green chiles
2 tablespoons chopped cilantro
1 tablespoon lime juice
1/2 teaspoon ground cumin
1/4 teaspoon ground red pepper
shredded Monterey Jack cheese

For the chicken, rub the chicken with the fajita seasoning. Brown in the heated olive oil in a skillet over medium-high heat for 3 minutes on each side or until cooked through. Remove the chicken to a platter and keep warm; reserve the drippings.

For the purée, drain the beans, reserving 2 tablespoons of the liquid; rinse and drain the beans.

Add the onion and garlic to the drippings in the skillet and sauté until tender. Combine with the beans, reserved bean liquid, tomatoes, cilantro, lime juice, cumin and red pepper in a blender or food processor container and process until smooth.

Spoon the bean mixture into a small saucepan and cook over medium heat until heated through. Sprinkle with cheese and serve with the chicken.

Serves two

Cookin' Cheap

Among Roanoke's shining stars is the nationally aired television show Cookin' Cheap. *Its creator, Laban Johnson, one of Roanoke's most colorful characters, was an avid fan of Julia Child.*

Admiration is not without limits, however, and when one of her recipes called for a French pickle that was expensive and hard to find, Laban fired back with Cookin' Cheap, *a show featuring recipes with easy-to-find and available ingredients.*

Laban presented the concept to Blue Ridge Public Television, and in 1980 it came to fruition. Today the show still features interesting dishes, in addition to comedy that could only come from the inevitable challenges facing the show's down-home, no-frills hosts, Larry Bly and Doug Patterson.

Chicken Stuffed with Spinach and Bleu Cheese

Spinach and Bleu Cheese Stuffing
$1/4$ cup finely chopped onion
$1/2$ teaspoon vegetable oil
4 garlic cloves, minced
$1/2$ cup thawed frozen chopped spinach
2 tablespoons crumbled bleu cheese
1 teaspoon Dijon mustard

Chicken
4 boneless skinless chicken breasts
$1/4$ teaspoon pepper
$1/2$ teaspoon vegetable oil
1 cup finely chopped onion
$1/3$ cup dry white wine
$1/2$ teaspoon dried thyme
1 cup reduced-sodium chicken broth
2 tablespoons Dijon mustard

For the stuffing, sauté the onion in the oil in a skillet over medium heat for 6 minutes or until tender. Add the garlic and sauté for 1 minute. Press the spinach to remove the excess moisture. Add the spinach to the skillet and sauté for 3 minutes. Combine with the bleu cheese and Dijon mustard in a small bowl and mix well.

For the chicken, cut a horizontal pocket in the thickest portion of each chicken breast. Spoon about 2 tablespoons of the stuffing mixture into each pocket; sprinkle with the pepper.

Heat the oil in a skillet over medium-high heat. Add the chicken and cook for 7 minutes on each side or until cooked through. Remove to a platter; reserve the drippings.

Add the onion to the drippings in the skillet and sauté for 5 minutes. Add the wine and thyme and cook for 3 minutes or until reduced by $1/2$. Stir in the chicken broth and Dijon mustard. Cook for 4 minutes or until slightly thickened.

Return the chicken to the skillet. Simmer, covered, for 2 minutes or until heated through.

Serves four

Thai Chicken with Basil

1 1/2 pounds boneless skinless chicken breasts
4 green onions
3 tablespoons peanut oil or vegetable oil
2 garlic cloves, minced
1 (1-inch) piece gingerroot, grated
1 tablespoon soy sauce
1 tablespoon lemon juice
2 teaspoons fish sauce
1 teaspoon sugar
1 or 2 serrano chiles, seeded, thinly sliced
4 fresh basil sprigs, coarsely chopped

Slice the chicken diagonally into 1/2-inch strips. Cut the white and pale green portions of the green onions into 1-inch pieces. Stir-fry the chicken in the heated oil in a wok or large sauté pan over medium-high heat for 2 to 3 minutes or until light brown. Remove with a slotted spoon.

Add the green onions, garlic and gingerroot to the wok and stir-fry over low heat for 1 minute or until aromatic. Add the soy sauce, lemon juice, fish sauce and sugar. Stir-fry for 1 minute. Add the serrano chiles, basil and chicken. Stir-fry until heated through. Serve with rice.

Serves four

Turkey Sautéed with Pears and Pecans

1 pound sliced turkey breast
2 garlic cloves, chopped
1 to 2 tablespoons olive oil
1 teaspoon cracked peppercorns
1/3 cup apple juice
2 tablespoons heavy cream
2 pears, sliced 1/4 inch thick
1/4 to 1/2 cup pecan halves, toasted

Sauté the turkey and garlic in heated olive oil in a skillet for 1 to 2 minutes or until brown; reduce the heat. Stir in the peppercorns, apple juice, heavy cream and pears. Cook for 1 to 2 minutes or until heated through, stirring frequently. Arrange on a serving platter. Garnish with the toasted pecans.

Serves four

The Asian Pantry

Fresh gingerroot: A little of this goes a long way. The root can be stored in the refrigerator for up to one month. It can also be grated and stored in the freezer, but it loses a bit of its punch.

Garlic: To save time, mince fresh garlic in quantity in the food processor. Place it in an airtight container, add enough olive oil to cover and store in the refrigerator. The infused oil is wonderful in salads. You can also buy minced garlic in the market.

Sesame Oil: The dark variety imparts a rich nutty flavor to foods.

Soy Sauce: Reduced-sodium soy sauce can be substituted for regular soy sauce without changing the flavor of the dish and is much better for you nutritionally.

Just Off the Appalachian Trail

On the outskirts of Roanoke lies a town unfamiliar to most people. For seasoned hikers and cyclists, however, Troutville is an oasis amidst the wilderness. Here two of America's most popular trails converge.

The 2000-mile Appalachian Trail and the 4500-mile TransAmerica Trail 76 bicycle route are traveled by people from all over the world. Many stop in Troutville, located just off the trails, for a well-earned respite or to collect their shipped supplies and mail at the post office or local inn. Trail Angels, local volunteers, are often found at these popular places to lend a helping hand to travelers in need.

★ *Sidebar Stars*

Susan Lazarus Bailey
Barbara Serrano "Bobbie" Black
Mary Elizabeth R. "Mimi" Coles
Laura Martin Davis

The Greenbrier's Peppered Maple Turkey Breast

Maple Syrup Glaze
1 cup West Virginia maple syrup
3 tablespoons light brown sugar
$1^1/2$ tablespoons Dijon mustard

Turkey
3 tablespoons cracked black peppercorns
1 tablespoon kosher salt
1 (3- to $3^1/2$-pound) boneless skinless turkey breast
$1/2$ cup (1 stick) butter, cut into 8 slices

For the glaze, combine the maple syrup, brown sugar and Dijon mustard in a small saucepan. Cook until the brown sugar dissolves, stirring constantly to blend well.

For the turkey, mix the peppercorns with the kosher salt in a shallow dish. Roll the turkey in the seasoning mixture, coating well. Place on a rack in a roasting pan; insert a meat thermometer into the thickest portion.

Roast at 325 degrees for 15 minutes; brush with the glaze. Roast for 5 minutes. Top with 4 slices of the butter. Roast for 15 minutes and brush again with the glaze. Roast for 5 minutes.

Place the remaining 4 slices butter on the turkey and roast for 15 minutes longer or to 150 degrees on the meat thermometer. Remove from the oven and brush again with the glaze; the turkey will continue to cook and should reach 160 degrees on the meat thermometer. Let stand for 15 minutes before carving into slices. Overlap the slices on a serving plate.

Combine the pan drippings with the remaining glaze in a small saucepan. Cook over high heat for 3 to 5 minutes or until slightly reduced. Spoon over the turkey slices. Serve warm or at room temperature.

Serves six to eight

Mustard and Horseradish Sauce

1/4 cup Dijon mustard
2 tablespoons prepared white horseradish
2/3 cup sour cream
2 tablespoons olive oil
2 tablespoons chopped fresh tarragon
salt and pepper to taste

Combine the Dijon mustard, horseradish, sour cream, olive oil and tarragon in a small bowl and mix well. Season with salt and pepper. Serve immediately or store, covered, in the refrigerator for up to 24 hours. Serve with beef.

Makes one cup

Tomato Béarnaise

4 shallots, minced
1 tablespoon (heaping) dried tarragon
1/3 cup tarragon vinegar
1/3 cup dry white wine
3 large egg yolks
2 1/2 tablespoons Dijon mustard
2 tablespoons fresh lemon juice
1 1/4 cups vegetable oil
1 cup olive oil
1/4 cup tomato paste
salt and freshly ground pepper to taste

Combine the shallots, tarragon, vinegar and wine in a small saucepan. Bring to a boil over high heat and cook until reduced to 1 tablespoon.

Process the egg yolks with the Dijon mustard and lemon juice in a food processor for 10 seconds. Add the vegetable oil and olive oil very gradually, processing constantly until thick and smooth.

Add the tomato paste and shallot reduction to the food processor container and process to mix well. Season with salt and pepper. Chill, covered, until ready to serve. Serve with meat, seafood, eggs and vegetables.

Makes three and one-half cups

Starfish

Fish & Seafood

Mountain Lake

    Tucked away near the summit of Bald Knob, one of the highest mountains in Virginia, is Mountain Lake, the location for the movie Dirty Dancing. *Accommodations are available in the grand stone hotel or in cottages nestled throughout the landscape overlooking the lake. One of only two natural lakes in Virginia, it is the highest lake east of the Rockies. Thousands of forested acres surround the area, providing seclusion to weary travelers now as in the past, when these woods served as hideouts for Tories and deserters from both sides during the Revolutionary War.*

    A wide variety of activities is available, ranging from archery to unique lawn games. While visitors may not find a lot of dirty dancing at Mountain Lake, they will find a delightful retreat.

**James River Equipment
Corporation**
Star Sponsor

Fish & Seafood

Stephen's Restaurant's Pistachio-Crusted Catfish with Tart Cider Butter Sauce

Stephen's enjoys its reputation as Roanoke's finest seafood restaurant.

Catfish
1 cup shelled pistachios
4 (4- to 5-ounce) catfish fillets or other white fish fillets
kosher salt to taste
2 tablespoons clarified butter or olive oil

Tart Cider Butter Sauce
1 cup heavy cream
2 tablespoons cider vinegar
2 tablespoons butter
salt and white pepper to taste

For the catfish, pulse the pistachios in a food processor just until chopped. Place in a shallow dish. Moisten the catfish fillets with water and coat lightly with the pistachios. Season lightly with kosher salt if using unsalted pistachios.

Spread the melted butter in a baking dish or nonstick baking pan. Arrange the catfish fillets in the prepared pan. Bake at 400 degrees for 10 to 15 minutes or until the fish flakes easily.

For the sauce, simmer the cream in a saucepan until reduced to 1/2 cup; the mixture should have the consistency of boiled custard. Stir in the vinegar. Remove from the heat and whisk in the butter. Season with salt and white pepper.

To serve, spoon the warm sauce onto serving plates and place the fish in the sauce. Serve with steamed spinach, asparagus or broccoli.

Serves four

Booker T. Washington

Booker Taliaferro Washington was born in 1856, a slave on the Burroughs' tobacco farm. At the age of nine, uneducated and newly freed, he left the farm. By the time he returned to the area in 1908, he was a college president and influential statesman. At his death in 1915, Booker T. Washington was an internationally prominent educator, author, and orator.

Washington frequently wrote and spoke of slave existence and the effect that experience had on his life. He was shaped not only by the realities of slave life, but also by the quest of African-Americans for education and equality, and the post-war struggle for political participation.

The original Burroughs' estate outside Roanoke is now a national monument. The park includes most of the original acreage as well as reconstructed farm buildings, and educates visitors as the great educator educated a people.

Lemony Stuffed Flounder

1/3 cup chopped celery
2 tablespoons chopped onion
1/3 cup butter
1 cup herb-seasoned stuffing mix
1 tablespoon chopped fresh parsley
1 tablespoon lemon juice
1 teaspoon grated lemon zest
1/4 teaspoon salt
1/4 teaspoon pepper
4 medium fresh flounder fillets or thawed frozen flounder fillets
1/3 cup butter
1/2 teaspoon dillweed

Sauté the celery and onion in 1/3 cup butter in a saucepan over medium heat. Add the stuffing mix, parsley, lemon juice, lemon zest, salt and pepper and mix well.

Cut the flounder fillets into halves and arrange 4 of the halves in an ungreased 9×9-inch baking dish. Spread the stuffing mixture over the fillet halves and top with the remaining halves.

Melt 1/3 cup butter in small saucepan and stir in the dillweed. Pour over the fish. Bake at 350 degrees on the center oven rack for 20 to 30 minutes or until the fish flakes easily.

Serves four

Red Snapper with Fresh Tomato Sauce

Light, but bursting with flavor.

1 small onion, chopped
1 garlic clove, chopped
2 tablespoons dry white wine
3 large tomatoes, chopped
1 teaspoon oregano
6 tablespoons dry white wine
2 (8-ounce) red snapper fillets
1/2 teaspoon oregano
1/2 teaspoon salt
pepper to taste

Spray a skillet with nonstick cooking spray. Add the onion, garlic and 2 tablespoons wine and cook over medium-low heat for 10 minutes or until the onion is tender, stirring occasionally. Add the tomatoes, 1 teaspoon oregano and 6 tablespoons wine. Simmer for 10 minutes or until reduced to a thick sauce.

Arrange the red snapper fillets in the sauce; sprinkle with 1/2 teaspoon oregano, salt and pepper. Simmer, covered, for 6 minutes or just until the fish is cooked through and flakes easily.

Serves two

Fillets of Salmon with Tomato and Cilantro Relish

Tomato and Cilantro Relish
1 cup chopped onion
6 tablespoons olive oil
2 tablespoons drained capers
4 cups chopped seeded peeled tomatoes
2 tablespoons grated lemon zest
1 teaspoon salt
$^1/_2$ teaspoon coarsely ground pepper
6 tablespoons chopped cilantro

Salmon
2 (1$^1/_4$-pound) salmon fillets
3 tablespoons fresh lemon juice
1 teaspoon Dijon mustard
$^1/_2$ teaspoon salt
$^1/_4$ teaspoon coarsely ground pepper
$^1/_2$ cup olive oil

Garnish
6 fresh cilantro sprigs

For the relish, sauté the onion in the olive oil in a heavy medium saucepan for 3 to 4 minutes or until translucent. Add the capers and tomatoes. Cook for 2 to 3 minutes. Season with the lemon zest, salt and pepper. Strain the mixture and discard the liquid. Combine the strained mixture with the cilantro in a bowl. Adjust the seasoning. Store, covered, in the refrigerator and return to room temperature before serving.

For the salmon, remove any bones that can be felt in the fish with tweezers. Place the fillets skin side down in a shallow dish. Combine the lemon juice, Dijon mustard, salt and pepper in a bowl and mix well. Whisk in the olive oil until smooth. Pour over the fillets. Marinate, covered, in the refrigerator for 2 hours or longer, turning several times.

Remove the fillets from the marinade and place skin side down on a rack in a broiler pan. Broil 5 to 6 inches from the heat source for 5 to 8 minutes or until the fillets flake easily.

To serve, cut each fillet into 3 serving pieces and place on serving plates. Top each with several tablespoonfuls of the Tomato and Cilantro Relish and garnish with cilantro. Serve with the remaining relish.

Serves six

The Homestead's Seafood Sauce

Serve this delicious sauce as an accompaniment with a seafood cocktail, baked crab meat, chilled poached salmon or as a dressing for your favorite seafood salad. For about 2$^1/_2$ cups of sauce whisk 2 cups homemade mayonnaise, 2$^2/_3$ tablespoons ketchup, 2$^2/_3$ tablespoons cocktail sauce, 2 tablespoons Cognac, 2 tablespoons vodka, 1 tablespoon chopped chutney, 1$^1/_2$ teaspoons lemon juice, 1$^1/_2$ teaspoons tarragon vinegar, 1$^1/_2$ teaspoons finely chopped fresh chives, 1$^1/_2$ teaspoons chopped fresh parsley, 1$^1/_2$ teaspoons minced celery and 1$^1/_2$ teaspoons chopped fresh tarragon in a bowl until well blended. Season with Tabasco sauce, salt and pepper. Serve immediately or store, covered, in the refrigerator for several days.

The Greenbrier's Pan-Roasted Salmon with Raspberry Mustard and Herb Crust

1/2 to 3/4 cup raspberry mustard or
    other whole-grain mustard
1 (3-pound) salmon fillet
1 tablespoon cracked black peppercorns

1 cup finely chopped fresh
    herbs, such as parsley, chives,
    dill and/or thyme

Spread the mustard over the salmon and sprinkle with the cracked pepper and fresh herbs. Cut into 6 to 8 equal portions. Spray a large ovenproof sauté pan with nonstick cooking spray or brush with a small amount of vegetable oil. Place the salmon skin side down in the pan. Cook over medium-high heat for 4 to 6 minutes.

Place the sauté pan in an oven heated to 450 degrees. Bake for 8 minutes or until the salmon is cooked through. Slide the spatula between the skin and the fillet to remove from the pan, leaving the skin in the pan.

Serves six to eight

Grilled Swordfish with Orange and Tomato Salsa

Orange and Tomato Salsa
3 oranges, peeled, chopped
1 1/2 cups chopped seeded tomatoes
1/3 cup minced onion
1/4 cup chopped fresh parsley
1 teaspoon minced gingerroot
2 garlic cloves, minced
2 tablespoons fresh orange juice
2 teaspoons balsamic vinegar
salt, cayenne pepper and black pepper
    to taste

Swordfish
3/4 cup teriyaki sauce
1/2 cup dry sherry
4 teaspoons minced garlic
2 teaspoons minced gingerroot
1 teaspoon sesame oil
6 (5- to 6-ounce) swordfish steaks,
    1 inch thick

For the salsa, combine the oranges, tomatoes, onion, parsley, gingerroot and garlic in a bowl. Add the orange juice, vinegar, salt, cayenne pepper and black pepper and toss to mix well. Let stand for 1 hour or store in the refrigerator until needed; return to room temperature to serve.

For the swordfish, combine the teriyaki sauce, wine, garlic, gingerroot and sesame oil in a saucepan. Bring to a boil, stirring frequently. Let cool. Pour into a shallow dish. Arrange the swordfish in the dish, turning to coat evenly. Marinate, covered, in the refrigerator for 1 1/2 hours, turning frequently.

Remove the fish from the marinade. Grill over medium-hot coals for 4 minutes on each side or until the fish flakes easily. Remove to a serving platter and serve with the salsa.

Serves six

Virginia Trout Meunière

1/4 cup milk
salt and pepper to taste
1/4 cup flour
4 trout fillets
1 tablespoon unsalted butter
1/4 cup vegetable oil
1/4 cup unsalted butter
1/2 cup pecan halves
2 tablespoons fresh lemon juice
2 tablespoons finely chopped fresh parsley

Combine the milk with salt and pepper to taste in a bowl and mix well. Mix the flour with salt and pepper to taste. Dip the trout in the milk mixture and coat with flour.

Melt 1 tablespoon butter with the oil in a heavy large skillet. Add the trout and sauté for 8 minutes on each side, basting frequently with the butter mixture. Remove to a warm platter; drain and wipe the skillet.

Sauté the pecans in 1/4 cup butter in a skillet until toasted. Add the lemon juice. Pour over the trout and sprinkle with the parsley.

Serves four

Simply Delicious Trout

3/4 cup flour
3 tablespoons salt
2 tablespoons black pepper
cayenne pepper to taste
2 pounds trout fillets
1 cup milk
3/4 cup fine bread crumbs
1 cup (2 sticks) butter, melted
1 cup sliced mushrooms
1 cup drained quartered artichoke hearts
2 tablespoons minced fresh parsley
1/4 cup dry white wine

Mix the flour, salt, black pepper and cayenne pepper in a bowl. Dip the trout in the milk and coat with the flour. Dip in the milk again and coat with the bread crumbs. Sauté the trout on both sides in the butter in a skillet; remove to a warm platter. Cook the mushrooms, artichokes and parsley in a saucepan over medium heat for 3 minutes or until heated through. Stir in the wine. Spoon over the trout.

Serves four

Original League Cookbook

Long before glossy four-color art cookbooks, before ISBN numbers and bar codes, before word processing, before Julia Child, there was the Junior League Cookbook. *Although what is presumed to be the sole remaining copy in existence bears no copyright information, League records mention its publication in the later 1920s or early 1930s. It is, as all cookbooks are, a reflection of the times and the cuisine of those times. After all, how many cookbooks today contain six recipes for Charlotte Russe, as well as recipes for Love Apples Grilled and Banana Mousse for Electric Refrigerator?*

Hot Off the Grill

Because of their texture, the following fish and shellfish are particularly suitable for grilling:

Grouper—a fish with firm flesh, sold as fillets and steaks. You may substitute sea bass or mahimahi for grouper.

Halibut—a white fish with firm flesh and a mild flavor, sold as fillets and steaks. It can be slightly more delicate than other fish categorized as firm and needs to be handled gently when turning on the grill.

Salmon—a fish with flesh ranging from pink to red and a range of flavor from mild to rich. It can take on a char and still keep its distinct flavor.

Swordfish—a mild, but distinctive-tasting, fish with a firm, meaty texture usually sold as steaks. Its natural oil content keeps it moist while grilling.

Tuna—a fish with deep red flesh that grills almost like a beef steak and almost never sticks to the grill. It is a good choice for the novice fish cook.

Scallops—a bivalve classified as either bay scallop or sea scallop. The larger sea scallop is more suitable for grilling because it has a meatier texture and can be easily skewered. They cook quickly, so watch closely on the grill.

Shrimp—large shrimp are best for grilling. They can be easily skewered and cook quickly.

Balsamic-Glazed Tuna

The Asian-inspired balsamic vinegar glaze stands up nicely to tuna.

4 (3/4-inch) tuna steaks
1/4 teaspoon salt
1 1/4 teaspoons freshly ground pepper
1 tablespoon balsamic vinegar
1/4 cup nonfat chicken broth
1 tablespoon reduced-sodium soy sauce
4 teaspoons dark brown sugar
1/2 teaspoon cornstarch
1/4 cup sliced green onions

Sprinkle the tuna with the salt and pepper. Spray a ridged skillet with nonstick cooking spray and heat over medium-high heat. Add the tuna and cook for 5 to 7 minutes on each side or until done to taste. Remove to a platter.

Combine the vinegar, chicken broth, soy sauce, brown sugar and cornstarch in a small saucepan and mix well. Bring to a boil and cook for 1 minute or until thickened, stirring constantly. Spoon over the tuna and sprinkle with the green onions.

Serves four

Pepper and Sesame Seared Tuna

4 (6- to 7-ounce) yellowfin tuna steaks
salt to taste
1 tablespoon coarsely cracked pepper
1 tablespoon sesame oil
2 tablespoons soy sauce
1/4 cup dry sherry
1/4 cup chopped fresh chives

Sprinkle the tuna steaks with salt and pepper, pressing gently to coat well. Heat the sesame oil in a large nonstick skillet over high heat. Add the steaks and cook for 3 minutes on each side or until seared and brown on the outside but just opaque in the center. Remove to a platter and tent loosely with foil to keep warm.

Add the soy sauce and wine to the skillet, stirring to deglaze the bottom. Simmer for 1 minute or until the mixture is slightly reduced. Spoon over the tuna and sprinkle with the chives.

Serves four

Top-Notch Crab Cakes

1 pound lump crab meat
2 tablespoons (heaping) mayonnaise
2 eggs, lightly beaten
2 slices bread, crumbled
1 small onion, chopped
1/4 green bell pepper, chopped
1/2 teaspoon Worcestershire sauce
garlic powder to taste
1/4 teaspoon dry mustard
1/4 teaspoon salt
1/2 teaspoon ground red pepper
butter or margarine

Combine the crab meat with the mayonnaise, eggs, bread crumbs, onion, bell pepper, Worcestershire sauce, garlic powder, dry mustard, salt and red pepper in a bowl and mix well. Chill, covered, in the refrigerator for 2 hours.

Shape into 4 patties. Sauté in butter in a skillet until golden brown on both sides.
Serves four

Classy Crab Quiche

1/2 cup mayonnaise or light mayonnaise
2 tablespoons flour
3 eggs, beaten
1/2 cup milk
6 ounces Swiss cheese, shredded
1/3 cup chopped green onions or onion
1 pound fresh or canned lump crab meat or backfin crab meat
1 baked pie shell, cooled

Combine the mayonnaise, flour, eggs, milk, cheese and green onions in a bowl and mix well. Fold in the crab meat gently. Spoon into the pie shell. Bake at 350 degrees for 40 to 45 minutes or until set.
Serves six

Succulent Scalloped Oysters

1 cup fine bread crumbs
1/4 cup (1/2 stick) butter, melted
1 quart fresh oysters, drained
2 tablespoons chopped fresh parsley
2 tablespoons chopped celery
1/2 teaspoon paprika
1 teaspoon salt
1 cup cream
1/4 cup white wine

Toss the bread crumbs with the butter in a small bowl. Arrange a single layer of oysters in a buttered baking dish and sprinkle with some of the bread crumbs, parsley, celery, paprika, salt and 2 tablespoons of the cream. Repeat the layers until all the ingredients are used, ending with bread crumbs. Pour the wine over the layers just before baking. Bake at 350 degrees for 20 minutes.

Serves six to eight

Special Lemon Scallops

This recipe won the sweepstakes in a 1975 Roanoke Times *favorite recipes contest. It has been a winner ever since.*

2 pounds sea scallops or bay scallops
2 tablespoons finely chopped onion
1/2 cup (1 stick) butter
1/2 cup sifted flour
1 cup chicken stock or chicken broth
1 cup sour cream
juice of 2 lemons
pepper to taste
hot buttered rice

Rinse the scallops and pat dry. Sauté with the onion in 2 tablespoons of the butter in a skillet for 5 minutes. Remove the scallop mixture to a baking dish and drain the skillet.

Melt the remaining 6 tablespoons butter in the skillet and stir in the flour. Cook until bubbly. Add the chicken stock and simmer over low heat until thickened, stirring constantly. Stir in the sour cream, lemon juice and pepper.

Pour the sauce over the scallops. Bake at 400 degrees for 10 to 15 minutes or until bubbly. Serve over rice.

Serves four to six

Grilled Shrimp and Scallop Skewers

3/4 cup dry white wine
1/3 cup soy sauce
1/3 cup packed brown sugar
2 teaspoons cornstarch
2 tablespoons vegetable oil
2 jalapeño peppers, minced
2 teaspoons grated gingerroot
2 garlic cloves, minced
juice of 2 limes
1/4 cup chopped cilantro
24 large uncooked shrimp, peeled, deveined
24 large uncooked sea scallops

Combine the wine, soy sauce, brown sugar and cornstarch in a small bowl; stir to dissolve the brown sugar and cornstarch completely. Heat the oil in a small saucepan over low heat. Add the jalapeño peppers, gingerroot and garlic. Cook, covered, for 6 minutes or until tender but not brown, stirring constantly. Stir in the wine mixture and increase the heat to medium-high. Cook until thickened, whisking constantly. Stir in the lime juice.

Cool the sauce to room temperature. Use immediately or let stand at room temperature for up to 4 hours. Reserve 1/2 cup of the sauce to serve with the shrimp. Stir the cilantro into the remaining sauce.

Thread 4 shrimp and 4 scallops alternately onto each of 6 metal skewers. Brush both sides with the sauce containing cilantro. Grill for 3 minutes on each side or just until cooked through. Remove to serving plates and serve with the reserved sauce.

Serves six

Science Museum

The latest wonders of science and technology unfold for all at the Science Museum. Occupying the fourth and fifth floors of Center in the Square, the museum is home to five permanent galleries and a variety of touring exhibits.

The quest for discovery starts in the Science Arcade, with displays of color, sound, and light, and in the Recollections Gallery, where time, space, and motion exist in a brilliant array of colors.

Budding physicists next become meteorologists in the state-of-the-art Weather Gallery, which includes a simulated tornado and weathercast equipment. Young scientists switch to marine biology at the Chesapeake Bay Touch Tank and human biology at Body Tech.

The Museum offers searches of the heavens at Hopkins Planetarium and special programming, such as summer camps, birthday parties, and an annual slumber party. It caters to and celebrates a child's insatiable thirst for knowledge from a child's eye view.

★ Sidebar Stars

Trudy and Robert Brailsford
Ruth Ellen and Paul Kuhnel
Shari and Tom Thomas
Sandra and Clark Worthy

Olives

Try some of the following varieties of olives to add flavor to cooking:

Kalamata—smooth dark olives with a pleasing aftertaste from Greece.

Manzanilla—traditional green cocktail olives with crisp flesh and a smoky flavor. Black Mission olives can be substituted in recipes.

Niçoise—small dark brown or purple olives with a sharp and slightly sour flavor. Because the pits are large in relation to the olive, there isn't much fruit left when they are pitted.

Oil-Cured—jet black and very wrinkled olives with the most astringent taste of all.

Shrimp and Feta with Pasta and Olives

1 1/2 pounds cooked shrimp, peeled, deveined
1 1/4 pounds feta cheese, crumbled
4 to 6 green onions, chopped
4 or 5 tomatoes, peeled, chopped
10 to 12 black olives, chopped
2 1/4 teaspoons oregano
salt and freshly ground pepper to taste
10 ounces uncooked pasta

Combine the shrimp, cheese, green onions, tomatoes, black olives, oregano, salt and pepper in a large bowl and mix well. Cook the pasta using the package directions; drain but do not rinse. Add to the shrimp mixture and toss lightly to mix. Let stand for 1 hour before serving at room temperature.

Serves six

Curried Shrimp and Rice

This combination of shrimp, rice, raisins, almonds and bacon in a casserole makes great party fare.

3 cups uncooked rice
1 large onion, chopped
1 cup (2 sticks) butter
2 teaspoons curry powder
salt and pepper to taste
5 pounds cooked shrimp, peeled, deveined
3/4 cup golden raisins
1/2 cup slivered almonds, toasted
1 pound bacon, crisp-fried, crumbled

Cook the rice using the package directions. Sauté the onion in the butter in a saucepan. Add the curry powder, salt and pepper and sauté until the curry powder is aromatic; remove from the heat. Add the rice, shrimp, raisins and almonds and mix well.

Spoon into a baking dish. Bake at 350 degrees until bubbly. Sprinkle with the bacon and serve with chutney and toasted coconut.

You may prepare this dish in advance and store in the refrigerator; increase the baking time if chilled.

Serves twelve

Sensational Shrimp and Bleu Cheese Grits

The bleu cheese adds a new dimension to this low-country classic.

3 cups milk
1 cup half-and-half
1 cup quick-cooking grits
1/2 medium onion, finely chopped
1 garlic clove, minced
3 tablespoons butter
1/2 to 1 cup crumbled bleu cheese, or to taste
1 tablespoon Worcestershire sauce
Tabasco sauce to taste
salt and pepper to taste
3 tablespoons butter
1 pound uncooked medium shrimp, peeled

Bring the milk and half-and-half just to a simmer in a large saucepan and stir in the grits. Cook for 5 to 10 minutes or until thick, stirring occasionally.

Sauté the onion and garlic in 3 tablespoons butter in a skillet for 5 minutes or until translucent but not brown. Add to the grits with the cheese, Worcestershire sauce, Tabasco sauce, salt and pepper and mix well. Keep warm.

Melt 3 tablespoons butter in the same skillet and add the shrimp. Sauté for 2 minutes on each side or just until cooked through. Spoon over the grits to serve.

Serves four to six

Shrimp with Red Bell Peppers and Zucchini

1 shallot, finely chopped
2 garlic cloves, finely chopped
3/4 cup (1 1/2 sticks) butter
12 ounces zucchini, sliced 1/2 inch thick
1/4 cup drained capers
2 pounds large uncooked shrimp, peeled
2 red bell peppers, roasted, cut into thin strips (see page 25)
1/3 cup chopped fresh basil
5 slices firm white bread, cut into 1/2-inch cubes

Sauté the shallot and garlic in the butter in a large skillet until the shallot is translucent. Add the zucchini and capers and sauté for 4 minutes. Stir in the shrimp and bell peppers.

Spoon into a 9×13-inch baking dish. Sprinkle with the basil and bread cubes. Bake at 350 degrees for 30 minutes or until the shrimp are cooked through and the bread cubes are brown.

You may prepare the dish in advance and store in the refrigerator for up to 8 hours before baking.

Serves six

Deveining Shrimp

It is not necessary to devein shrimp, as the vein is harmless, but it is easy to remove if you prefer, and you don't need a fancy deveining gadget. Just grasp the tail of the shrimp in one hand and gently remove the shell and tail. Pinch the vein at the tail end of the shrimp and pull it out. You can also make a tiny slit along the back of the shrimp with a sharp paring knife and lift out the vein with the tip of the knife.

Sautéed Shrimp in Béchamel Sauce

Serve in patty shells or over sautéed spinach, pasta or rice.

Shrimp
$1^1/2$ cups sliced fresh mushrooms
2 tablespoons butter
Worcestershire sauce and Tabasco sauce to taste
$1/4$ teaspoon paprika
garlic salt and white pepper to taste
$1^1/2$ pounds uncooked shrimp, peeled, deveined
1 tablespoon chicken stock
$1/4$ cup dry sherry

Béchamel Sauce
$1^1/2$ cups milk
2 to 3 tablespoons chopped shallots
2 tablespoons chopped celery
2 bay leaves
6 whole peppercorns
3 tablespoons flour
3 tablespoons butter
1 tablespoon chopped fresh parsley
1 egg yolk, beaten

For the shrimp, sauté the mushrooms in the butter in a saucepan. Stir in the Worcestershire sauce, Tabasco sauce, paprika, garlic salt and white pepper. Add the shrimp and chicken stock and cook just until the shrimp are opaque. Add the sherry. Keep the mixture warm.

For the sauce, combine the milk, shallots, celery, bay leaves and peppercorns in a small saucepan. Heat over low heat just until the mixture steams. Strain into a bowl.

Whisk the flour into the melted butter in a saucepan and cook until bubbly. Add the strained milk and cook until thickened, whisking constantly. Add the parsley. Whisk a small amount of the hot mixture into the egg yolk; whisk the egg yolk into the hot mixture.

Pour the sauce over the shrimp. Cook until heated through, but do not boil; add a small amount of additional milk if the mixture appears too thick.

Serves four to six

Pan-Fried Shrimp and Chicken with Penne

2 eggs
2 cups French bread crumbs
1/4 cup chopped fresh parsley
1/2 teaspoon salt
1/2 teaspoon black pepper
12 ounces boneless skinless chicken breasts
1/4 cup olive oil
8 ounces uncooked large shrimp, peeled, deveined
3/4 cup white wine
1 cup heavy cream
1/4 cup grated Parmesan cheese
cayenne pepper to taste
8 ounces uncooked penne or other pasta

Garnish
2 tablespoons chopped fresh parsley

Beat the eggs in a shallow dish. Mix the bread crumbs, parsley, salt and black pepper in a separate shallow dish. Dip the chicken into the eggs and coat with the bread crumb mixture.

Heat 3 tablespoons of the olive oil in a heavy large skillet over medium-high heat. Add the chicken and sauté for 4 minutes on each side or until cooked through. Remove to a plate and cut into 1/2-inch pieces. Drain the skillet.

Heat the remaining 1 tablespoon olive oil in the skillet and add the shrimp. Sauté over medium-high heat for 3 minutes or just until cooked through. Remove to the plate with the chicken with a slotted spoon.

Add the wine to the skillet, stirring to deglaze. Cook for 2 minutes or until reduced to 1/2 cup. Add the cream and cook for 3 minutes or until slightly thickened. Stir in the cheese and cayenne pepper. Return the chicken and shrimp with any accumulated juices to the skillet.

Cook the pasta using the package directions. Drain and add to the chicken and shrimp mixture in the skillet; toss to mix well. Adjust the seasonings. Spoon into a serving bowl and garnish with parsley.

Serves four

Summertime Grilled Shrimp

Southeastern Asia meets southwestern Virginia in this incredibly delicious summer entrée.

Ginger Sesame Vinaigrette
1/2 cup rice wine vinegar
2 tablespoons sesame oil
2 tablespoons soy sauce
2 tablespoons fresh lime juice
2 tablespoons minced gingerroot
2 tablespoons coarsely chopped cilantro
1 garlic clove, minced
1 fresh chile, minced
2 tablespoons sugar

Grilled Shrimp and Salad
1 pound uncooked medium shrimp, peeled, deveined
1 tablespoon vegetable oil
salt and pepper to taste
2 cucumbers
1 carrot
1 red bell pepper, coarsely chopped
4 scallions, coarsely chopped with some of the tops
salt and pepper to taste

For the vinaigrette, combine the vinegar, sesame oil, soy sauce, lime juice, gingerroot, cilantro, garlic, chile and sugar in a bowl and whisk to mix well.

For the shrimp and salad, thread the shrimp onto skewers; brush lightly with the oil and sprinkle with salt and pepper. Grill over medium-hot coals for 3 to 4 minutes on each side.

Peel the cucumbers and carrot. Cut the cucumbers into halves lengthwise and cut into thin strips. Cut the carrot into halves crosswise and cut into thin strips. Combine the cucumbers and carrot with the bell pepper and scallions in a bowl. Add the vinaigrette and toss to mix well. Season with salt and pepper.

Spoon the cucumber mixture onto serving plates. Remove the shrimp from the skewers and arrange over the salad.

Serves four

Grilled Shrimp Olé

Cilantro Lime Dressing
3/4 cup olive oil
5 tablespoons fresh lime juice
6 tablespoons chopped fresh cilantro
1 1/2 tablespoons minced seeded jalapeño pepper
2 teaspoons ground cumin
salt and pepper to taste

Grilled Shrimp and Tostada Salad
3 cups chopped seeded tomatoes
1 (15-ounce) can black beans, rinsed, drained
3/4 cup chopped green onions
3/4 cup chopped cilantro
3/4 cup chopped red onion
2 ears of corn, husked
24 large shrimp, peeled with tails intact, deveined
6 cups (or more) shredded lettuce
salt and pepper to taste
24 large tortilla chips

Garnish
chopped cilantro

For the dressing, whisk the olive oil into the lime juice in a medium bowl. Add the cilantro, jalapeño pepper and cumin and whisk until smooth. Season with salt and pepper. Reserve 1/4 cup of the dressing for grilling. Let the remaining dressing stand, covered, for up to 6 hours.

For the shrimp and salad, combine the tomatoes, beans, green onions, cilantro and onion in a large bowl and toss lightly. Chill, covered, in the refrigerator for up to 6 hours.

Brush the corn with some of the reserved dressing. Grill over medium-high heat for 5 minutes or until it begins to brown, turning frequently. Brush the shrimp with the remaining reserved dressing. Grill for 5 minutes or until the shrimp are opaque, turning occasionally.

Cut the kernels from the corn and add to the tomato mixture. Add the lettuce and enough of the remaining dressing to coat well and toss to mix. Season with salt and pepper. Spoon onto serving plates and top with the shrimp. Arrange the tortilla chips around the salad and garnish with cilantro.

Serves four

Storing Shrimp

Fresh shrimp are very perishable and should be cooked within two days of their purchase. To store, rinse the shrimp under cold running water and pat dry with paper towels. Cover loosely with waxed paper to allow for the circulation of air and place on a bed of ice. Store in the refrigerator. Shrimp can also be frozen but it loses some of its texture when thawed.

Star Grazing

Vegetables & Side Dishes

To Market, To Market

The market is the heart of Roanoke's resurgent downtown. It is the oldest continuously operating farmers' market in Virginia and a weekly pilgrimage for many. Everything there is richly hued and full of the promise of the season, even in winter, when the aroma of roasting chestnuts beckons celebrants to a Dickens of a Christmas. On cold, clear, starlit nights, carolers and Father Christmas in Victorian garb stroll the streets, avoiding the queue for horse-drawn carriage rides.

Spring visitors delight in the thaw and the delicate celadon of asparagus and peas, the rich purple of pansies, and anything required to bring a garden to life.

Summer brings a vast assortment of freshly picked produce, the heady scent of flowers and herbs, and rich colors—the crimson of tomatoes and peppers, the sage of Blue Lake green beans, the striated hunter green of cucumbers, the pale moonlight of Silver Queen corn, and the incomparable orange-red of peaches.

Autumn, in all its glory, provides welcome respite from the heat, indescribably sweet crisp apples, and a view of the tapestry that is the Blue Ridge.

The market is home, too, to a wide assortment of artisans who ply their crafts and sell their wares at a number of unique shops, galleries, and restaurants, including many across the street in the Market Building. There, visitors can also choose from a variety of ethnic cuisines or simple hamburgers and hot dogs.

Valley Investors Corporation
Star Sponsor

Vegetables & Side Dishes

Asparagus with Vinaigrette

Be sure not to overcook the asparagus; it should be slightly crisp for the best results.

1 to 1 1/2 pounds fresh asparagus, trimmed
1/4 cup white wine vinegar
2 tablespoons Dijon mustard
1 tablespoon chopped chives
2 tablespoons minced shallots or green onions
2 tablespoons chopped fresh parsley
1 teaspoon chopped fresh tarragon
2 hard-cooked eggs, chopped
3/4 cup olive oil

Cook the asparagus in a small amount of water in a saucepan until tender-crisp; drain and chill in the refrigerator. Combine the vinegar, Dijon mustard, chives, shallots, parsley, tarragon and eggs in a bowl. Add the olive oil and whisk to mix well. Serve over the asparagus.

Serves six

Green Beans with Balsamic Pesto

1/4 cup extra-virgin olive oil
1 large garlic clove
1 1/3 cups packed fresh basil leaves
3/4 cup grated Parmesan cheese
salt and pepper to taste
1 1/2 pounds fresh green beans, trimmed
4 to 5 tablespoons balsamic vinegar
1/2 teaspoon dark brown sugar

Combine the olive oil and garlic in a food processor or blender container and process until nearly smooth. Add the basil and cheese and process until the basil is chopped but not puréed. Season with salt and pepper. Let stand, covered, at room temperature until ready to use.

Bring 2 inches of water to a boil in a 6-quart steamer. Place the beans in the steamer basket and steam, covered, for 6 minutes or until tender-crisp. Combine the hot beans with the basil mixture in a bowl. Blend the vinegar with the brown sugar in a small bowl and add to the beans; toss to coat well. Adjust the seasonings. Serve warm or at room temperature; do not refrigerate before serving.

Serves six to eight

Virginia's Explore Park

Venture off the Blue Ridge Parkway into Roanoke's own version of Brigadoon— Virginia's Explore Park. Time stands still as visitors journey back in history. Original and reconstructed buildings from 1671 to 1850 provide the setting for interpretations of Native American folkways and colonial frontier culture.

For those ready to return to the 21st century, hiking and mountain biking trails, bateau rides, and fishing on the Roanoke River await, as does the opportunity to enjoy a variety of flora and fauna. Top it off by dining at the authentic 19th-century Brugh Tavern.

★ *Sidebar Stars*

Jane Eggleston Coulter
Jan Butler Garrett
Kay Johnson Kelly
Betty Hardt Lesko

How to Keep a Tomato

To preserve the flavor of ripe tomatoes and to ripen green tomatoes, do not place them in the refrigerator. If, however, you want to use tomatoes green, place them in the refrigerator to inhibit the ripening process.

Fresh Green Beans with Tomatoes and Garlic

2 pounds fresh green beans
1 medium onion, thinly sliced
2 tablespoons olive oil
3 garlic cloves, minced
1 (29-ounce) can tomatoes, drained, chopped
1 (14-ounce) can tomatoes, drained, chopped
1 teaspoon sugar
salt and freshly ground pepper to taste

Garnish
3 or 4 slices bacon, crisp-fried, crumbled
grated Parmesan cheese

Trim the green beans and cut into halves. Cook in water to cover in a saucepan for 8 to 10 minutes or until tender-crisp. Drain and rinse under cold water until cool; drain well.

Sauté the onion in the heated olive oil in a large sauté pan for 5 minutes. Add the garlic and sauté for 1 minute. Add the green beans and toss to coat well. Add the tomatoes, sugar, salt and pepper.

Bring to a boil and reduce the heat. Simmer, covered, for 10 minutes. Cook, uncovered, for 1 or 2 minutes longer or until the liquid is slightly reduced. Garnish with bacon and Parmesan cheese.

You may prepare this in advance and reheat to serve.
Serves six

Mixed Bean Casserole

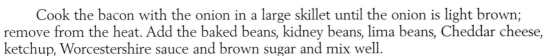

4 slices bacon, chopped
1 medium onion, chopped
1 (16-ounce) can baked beans in tomato sauce, drained
1 (16-ounce) can kidney beans, drained
1 (16-ounce) can lima beans, drained
1 cup cubed sharp Cheddar cheese
1/3 cup ketchup
2 teaspoons Worcestershire sauce
1/2 cup packed brown sugar
grated Parmesan cheese

Cook the bacon with the onion in a large skillet until the onion is light brown; remove from the heat. Add the baked beans, kidney beans, lima beans, Cheddar cheese, ketchup, Worcestershire sauce and brown sugar and mix well.

Spoon into a greased shallow baking dish and sprinkle with Parmesan cheese. Bake at 350 degrees for 30 minutes.

Serves six

Cognac Carrots

Even those who think they don't like carrots will love this heady mix.

1 pound peeled baby carrots
sugar and salt to taste
1/4 cup (1/2 stick) butter
2 to 3 teaspoons sugar
2 tablespoons Cognac

Combine the carrots with sugar and salt to taste in a saucepan. Add water to just cover and cook until tender; drain. Melt the butter in a skillet and add the carrots. Sprinkle with 2 to 3 teaspoons sugar and cook over low heat until heated through. Add the Cognac and serve immediately.

Serves four to six

Cabbage and Potatoes with
Tomatoes and Smoked Cheese

*This is hearty enough to serve as a main dish, especially for a
cold-weather supper.*

4 medium red potatoes
4 cups finely chopped green cabbage
2 tablespoons water
3 medium tomatoes
1 tablespoon olive oil
2 or 3 garlic cloves, minced
2 teaspoons oregano
$^1/_2$ teaspoon crushed rosemary
$^1/_2$ teaspoon dill
salt and freshly ground pepper to taste
1 cup shredded smoked Cheddar cheese

Cook the unpeeled potatoes in water to cover in a large saucepan over medium-high heat for 15 to 20 minutes or until tender but still firm. Drain and rinse in a colander and cool.

Combine the cabbage with 2 tablespoons water in a saucepan. Cook, covered, over low heat for 5 minutes or just until the cabbage wilts; drain any liquid that does not evaporate.

Seed and chop the tomatoes and combine with the olive oil, garlic, oregano, rosemary, dill, salt and pepper in a large bowl. Add the cabbage and toss to mix well.

Cut the potatoes into bite-size pieces. Add to the cabbage mixture with the cheese and mix gently. Spoon into a baking dish coated with olive oil. Bake, covered, at 375 degrees for 25 to 30 minutes or until the casserole is heated through and the cheese melts. Serve immediately.

Serves eight as a side dish or four as a main dish

Best Ever Corn Pudding

The topping of butter, brown sugar and cinnamon is the secret step in this delicious corn pudding.

6 ears fresh corn
6 tablespoons (3/4 stick) butter
2 tablespoons sugar
2 tablespoons (scant) flour
1/2 cup light cream
4 eggs, beaten
1 1/2 teaspoons baking powder
2 tablespoons brown sugar
1/4 teaspoon cinnamon
2 tablespoons butter or margarine, melted

Cut the corn from the ears and measure 4 cups and set aside.

Melt 6 tablespoons butter with the sugar in a saucepan. Stir in the flour and cook until bubbly; remove from the heat. Add the cream gradually. Stir in the eggs and baking powder and mix well. Mix in the corn.

Spoon into a buttered 1 1/2-quart baking dish. Bake at 350 degrees for 45 minutes or until a knife inserted in the center comes out clean.

Mix the brown sugar and cinnamon in a small bowl. Drizzle 2 tablespoons melted butter over the pudding and sprinkle with the brown sugar mixture. Bake for 5 minutes longer.

You may substitute two drained 12-ounce cans of yellow or white corn kernels for the fresh corn if you prefer.

Serves six to eight

Vegetable Complements

Artichokes—dill, curry powder, or mustard
Asparagus—dill or nutmeg
Beets—mustard, ginger, or caraway
Broccoli—nutmeg, oregano, or paprika
Brussels Sprouts—dill, mustard, or celery seeds
Cabbage—curry powder, dill, or celery seeds
Carrots—anise, chives, or dill
Cauliflower—tarragon, cilantro, rosemary, or cumin
Corn—cumin, sage, or chili powder
Cucumber—dill, basil, mint, or chives
Eggplant—curry powder, basil, or oregano
Green beans—tarragon, ginger, or dill
Leeks—rosemary, mustard, or tarragon
Mushrooms—thyme, paprika, or nutmeg
Onions—sorrel, fennel seeds, or curry powder
Peas—mint, tarragon, or ginger
Peppers—thyme, oregano, or cumin
Potatoes—dill, parsley, caraway, or chives
Spinach—nutmeg, mustard, or oregano
Summer squash—basil, cilantro, or anise seeds
Sweet potatoes—cinnamon, cloves, nutmeg, or ginger

Fresh Corn on the Cob

Combine 5 quarts water with 1/4 teaspoon sugar and the juice of 1 lemon in a large saucepan and bring to a boil. Add 6 ears of corn and cook for 8 to 10 minutes or until tender. Salt the corn after it is cooked, as adding salt to the cooking water will cause it to be tough.

Grilled Corn with Chili Butter

1/2 cup olive oil
1/2 cup lime juice
1/2 cup (1 stick) butter, melted
2 tablespoons chili powder
1 teaspoon crushed red pepper
salt to taste
12 ears of corn, husked

Combine the olive oil, lime juice, butter, chili powder, crushed red pepper and salt in a bowl and mix well. Brush over the corn. Grill until tender, brushing frequently with the butter mixture.

You may also place the corn ears on squares of foil, drizzle with the butter mixture, seal and grill until tender.

Serves twelve

Roasted Onions with Balsamic Glaze

This is good served with the Beef Tenderloin with Herb and Garlic Crust on page 66.

4 pounds medium red onions
1/4 cup olive oil
salt and pepper to taste
6 tablespoons (3/4 stick) butter
3 tablespoons sugar
6 tablespoons balsamic vinegar

Garnish
1 tablespoon chopped fresh parsley

Cut the onions through the stem ends into 3/4-inch wedges. Toss with the olive oil in a bowl. Arrange cut side down on 2 foiled-lined baking sheets and sprinkle with salt and pepper. Place 1 baking sheet on the center rack of an oven preheated to 500 degrees. Place the other baking sheet on a rack in the lower third of the oven. Roast for 45 minutes or until the onions are brown and tender, turning once.

Melt the butter in a heavy small saucepan and stir in the sugar until dissolved. Remove from the heat and stir in the vinegar. Simmer for 2 minutes or until thickened.

Arrange the onions on a platter and drizzle with the glaze. Garnish with the parsley.

Serves ten

Caramelized Onion Tart

3 pounds large sweet onions, sliced
2 tablespoons olive oil
1 teaspoon salt
1 sheet frozen puff pastry, thawed
$1/2$ cup grated Parmesan cheese

Garnish
fresh rosemary sprigs

Cook the onions in the olive oil in a large skillet over low heat for 30 to 35 minutes or until caramel color, stirring frequently. Stir in the salt.

Fit the puff pastry into a 9-inch square tart pan and trim the edge. Bake at 400 degrees for 15 to 20 minutes or until brown. Press the pastry with the back of a spoon to flatten.

Spoon the onions into the tart shell and sprinkle with the cheese. Bake for 5 minutes longer. Garnish with fresh rosemary.

Serves six

Sugar Snap Peas with Carrot Buttons

1 pound sugar snap peas
2 cups ($1/4$-inch) carrot slices
3 cups chicken broth
1 tablespoon butter
salt and freshly ground pepper to taste

Rinse the peas; remove and discard the ends and strings. Combine the carrots with the chicken broth in a 10- or 12-inch skillet. Cook, covered, for 4 minutes or until tender-crisp. Add the peas. Cook, covered, for 2 to 3 minutes or just until tender, stirring once; drain.

Melt the butter in a large skillet. Add the peas and carrots and cook over medium-high heat until heated through. Season with salt and pepper.

Serves eight

The Merchant of Basil

One stall at the Market is occasionally tenanted by an Italian merchant with a deep and abiding love of exotic field greens and bunches upon bunches of extravagantly leaved, beautifully glossy and pungent basil. His garden space is a small, but highly productive, plot near Hollins that is seemingly unscathed by drought, pestilence, or disease.

In late summer, it is impossible to resist bringing home great grocery bags full of the basil. It demands the finest ingredients and an occasional new twist, and one of the best is Roasted Garlic Pesto (at right).

The Merchant of Basil Roasted Garlic Pesto

1 garlic bulb
1 teaspoon olive oil
2 cups fresh basil leaves
1/4 cup grated first-quality Parmesan cheese
1/4 cup pine nuts
1/4 cup (1/2 stick) butter, softened
2 tablespoons olive oil
1 tablespoon lemon juice

Cut the top off the whole garlic bulb and place it on a sheet of foil. Drizzle with 1 teaspoon olive oil; fold the foil around the garlic and seal. Roast at 425 degrees for 30 minutes. Cool to room temperature and squeeze the cloves from the skins into a food processor container.

Add the basil, cheese, pine nuts, butter, 2 tablespoons olive oil and lemon juice and process until smooth, scraping the side of the container occasionally.

Makes two cups

Mashed Potatoes with Green Chiles and Roasted Garlic

4 garlic cloves
olive oil
4 large russet potatoes
1 teaspoon salt
1/2 cup milk
2 tablespoons drained and chopped canned green chiles
1/4 cup (1/2 stick) unsalted butter, melted
salt and freshly ground pepper to taste

Remove and discard the outer skin of the garlic cloves and place on a square of foil. Drizzle with olive oil, wrap loosely in the foil and seal. Bake at 400 degrees for 25 to 30 minutes or until tender. Cool to room temperature and press the garlic from the skins and chop.

Peel the potatoes and cut into 1-inch pieces. Combine with 1 teaspoon salt and cold water to cover in a saucepan. Cook over medium-high heat for 15 minutes or until tender; drain.

Combine the potatoes with the milk in a large bowl and mash with a potato masher. Add the green chiles, roasted garlic and butter. Beat with a mixer until smooth. Season with salt and pepper to taste.

You may roast entire heads of garlic in this manner.

Serves four to six

Corned Beef & Co.'s Sharp Cheddar Smashed Red-Skinned Potatoes

7 pounds red-skinned potatoes
1 cup (2 sticks) butter, softened
2 cups milk
1 cup sour cream
2 cups shredded sharp Cheddar cheese
1 bunch green onions, sliced
3 tablespoons southwest-flavor seasoning
3 tablespoons salt
3 tablespoons pepper

Steam the potatoes in a small amount of water in a large saucepan until tender. Place in large bowl.

Combine the butter, milk, sour cream, cheese, green onions, southwest seasoning, salt and pepper in a small saucepan. Bring just to a boil, stirring to mix well. Add to the potatoes and mash until smooth, adding additional milk or sour cream if necessary for the desired consistency.

Serves eight

Horseradish Mashed Potatoes

8 medium russet potatoes, peeled, chopped
salt to taste
5 tablespoons butter or margarine
1 teaspoon salt
milk
3/4 cup sour cream
3 tablespoons prepared horseradish

Cook the potatoes in salted water in a saucepan for 20 to 25 minutes or until very tender; drain. Mash until smooth, adding the butter, 1 teaspoon salt and enough milk to make of the desired consistency. Add the sour cream and horseradish and mix with an electric mixer until fluffy.

Serves eight

Roasted Potato Wedges

Cut medium baking potatoes into wedges and coat with ranch salad dressing. Arrange on a baking sheet and roast at 425 degrees for 30 minutes or until tender, turning once. Season with pepper. Serve with a mixture of $1/2$ cup ranch salad dressing, $1/4$ cup sour cream and $1/4$ cup salsa.

Layered Potato and Tomato Tart

2 tablespoons butter
2 tablespoons olive oil
1 cup thinly sliced onion
2 garlic cloves, minced
2 pounds tomatoes, thinly sliced
2 tablespoons chopped fresh parsley
$1/2$ teaspoon dried basil
$1/2$ teaspoon dried oregano
$1^1/2$ teaspoons salt
pepper to taste
$2^1/2$ pounds potatoes, peeled, thinly sliced
1 cup shredded Swiss cheese
$1/4$ cup grated Parmesan cheese
2 tablespoons butter

Melt 2 tablespoons butter with the olive oil in a skillet. Add the onion and garlic and sauté until translucent but not brown. Add the tomatoes, parsley, basil, oregano, salt and pepper and mix gently. Spoon $1/3$ of the mixture into a buttered 3-quart baking dish.

Layer the potatoes, Swiss cheese, Parmesan cheese and remaining tomato mixture $1/2$ at a time in the prepared dish. Dot with 2 tablespoons butter. Bake at 375 degrees for $1^1/2$ hours or until the potatoes are tender.

Serves eight

Spinach Sauté

1 pound fresh spinach
2 tablespoons olive oil
2 tablespoons dry white wine
$1/4$ cup grated Parmesan cheese

Rinse the spinach; remove and discard the stems and pat the leaves dry. Sauté in the olive oil in a large skillet over high heat for 30 seconds or until the spinach wilts. Add the wine and cook until the liquid evaporates. Sprinkle with the cheese and serve immediately.

Serves one

Tomato Relish

This colorful relish is beautiful in ordinary jars and makes a wonderful gift.

3 pounds tomatoes, peeled, cut into quarters
2 bunches scallions, diagonally sliced
4 serrano or jalapeño peppers
1½ tablespoons mustard seeds
⅔ cup grated gingerroot
10 garlic cloves, minced
3 tablespoons ground cumin
1 tablespoon paprika
½ teaspoon ground turmeric
1½ tablespoons crushed pepper
1½ cups olive oil
1½ cups rice wine vinegar
¾ cup packed brown sugar
1½ tablespoons salt

Combine the tomatoes, scallions and peppers in a glass dish and mix gently.
Mix the mustard seeds, gingerroot, garlic, cumin, paprika, turmeric and pepper in
a small bowl.

Heat the olive oil in a skillet until smoking. Add the spice mixture and stir-fry for
2 to 3 minutes. Add to the tomato mixture and mix well.

Combine the vinegar, brown sugar and salt in a small saucepan. Bring to a boil and
pour over the tomato mixture. Let stand until cool. Chill, covered, in the refrigerator for
2 days before serving.

Serves twenty

Deep-Dish Tomato Pie

A savory way to show off fresh summer beefsteak tomatoes.

3 large tomatoes, thickly sliced, drained
1 baked (9-inch) deep-dish pie shell, cooled
4 green onions, chopped
chopped fresh basil
chopped fresh chives
salt and pepper to taste
1 cup mayonnaise
1 cup shredded sharp Cheddar cheese

Layer the tomatoes in the pie shell, sprinkling each layer with green onions, basil,
chives, salt and pepper. Combine the mayonnaise and cheese in a bowl and mix well.
Spread over the tomatoes. Bake at 350 degrees for 30 minutes.

Serves four to six

Zucchini Fritters

An unusual accompaniment that will go with many different main dishes.

2 (8-ounce) zucchini, trimmed
salt to taste
1 egg
2 tablespoons heavy cream
1 tablespoon flour
2 garlic cloves, minced
2 to 4 tablespoons corn oil

Grate the zucchini or shred in a food processor. Layer in a strainer over a bowl, sprinkling each layer with salt. Let stand for 30 minutes, pressing occasionally to remove the liquid. Squeeze any remaining liquid from the zucchini.

Combine the egg, cream, flour and garlic in a medium bowl and whisk to mix well. Add the zucchini and mix well; the egg mixture will just coat the zucchini.

Heat 2 tablespoons of the corn oil in a large skillet or nonstick griddle. Spoon the zucchini mixture into the skillet by heaping tablespoonfuls and press with the back of the spoon to flatten. Cook until brown on both sides, turning once and pressing with the spoon to flatten; add the remaining 2 tablespoons of oil if necessary. Drain on paper towels and serve immediately.

Makes eight to ten

Zippy Zucchini

Even children love this.

1/4 cup (1/2 stick) butter
2 tablespoons olive oil
2 pounds small zucchini, sliced
2 medium red onions, sliced
2 garlic cloves, cut into halves
2 teaspoons cider vinegar
2 teaspoons lemon juice
1/2 teaspoon salt
1/2 teaspoon pepper
3 tablespoons grated Parmesan cheese

Heat the butter with the olive oil in a large skillet over medium heat. Add the zucchini and sauté until light brown on both sides. Remove from the skillet. Drain on paper towels. Add the onions and half the garlic to the skillet and sauté until tender. Remove with a slotted spoon.

Oil a 2-quart baking dish with additional olive oil and rub with the remaining garlic halves. Layer half the zucchini, the onion mixture and the remaining zucchini in the prepared dish.

Add the vinegar, lemon juice, salt and pepper to the skillet. Cook until heated through, stirring constantly. Pour over the layers and sprinkle with the cheese. Bake at 350 degrees for 20 to 25 minutes or until golden brown.

Serves six to eight

Winter Squash with Chard and Tomatoes

Mediterranean seasonings add an unusual touch to this traditional fall vegetable.

2 tablespoons pine nuts
1 (1$\frac{1}{4}$-pound) acorn squash, peeled
1 large red onion
1 pound Swiss chard
1 tablespoon olive oil
3 garlic cloves, minced
2 teaspoons oregano
$\frac{1}{4}$ teaspoon red chile flakes
$\frac{1}{2}$ teaspoon salt
1$\frac{1}{4}$ cups vegetable stock
8 ounces fresh pear tomatoes, chopped
2 tablespoons balsamic vinegar

Sprinkle the pine nuts into a heavy skillet. Cook over medium-high heat until light brown and aromatic, shaking the pan to prevent scorching. Mince and set aside.

Cut the squash into halves and discard the seeds. Chop the squash and onion coarsely. Rinse the chard; remove and reserve the stems. Heat the olive oil in a heavy large skillet. Add the garlic, oregano and chile flakes. Sauté for 1 minute. Add the squash, onion, reserved chard stems and salt. Cook, covered, for 5 minutes.

Add the vegetable stock and cook, covered, for 7 minutes. Stir in the tomatoes. Cook, covered, for 5 minutes longer, stirring frequently.

Place the undrained chard leaves in a saucepan. Cook over medium-low heat for 5 minutes or until wilted. Spoon onto serving plates. Stir the vinegar gently into the squash mixture. Spoon over the chard and sprinkle with the pine nuts.

Serves six

Cyberchef

With the advent of the information age, many exotic resources are just a .com away. Precede the following site names with the ubiquitous "www.":
akagourmet.com
bonappetit.com
chefsanborn.com
cooking.com
cybercucina.com
deananddeluca.com
e-java.com
epicurious.com
food.com
foodtv.com
fultonstreet.com
globalgourmet.com
gourmet.com
gourmetbaskets.net
gourmetchocolate.com
gourmetexpo.com
gourmettrader.com
gourmetworld.com
gourmet-world.com
greatfood.com
igourmet.com
internetcookbook.com
lazygourmet.com
mustardstore.com
nycfood.com
onlinefood.com
saguarofood.com
send.com
southerngourmetfoods.com
southernseason.com
suttongourmet.com
tavolo.com
wine.com

Compound Butters

*For Mustard Butter, add
2 teaspoons Dijon mustard to
1/2 cup softened unsalted butter.*

*For Garlic Butter or Shallot
Butter, blanch 3 garlic cloves
or 1/2 cup chopped shallots for
2 minutes and process with
1/2 cup melted butter in a food
processor. Chill until firm.*

*For Herb Butter, blanch
1/4 cup fresh herbs for
2 minutes and drain. Purée
with 1/2 cup melted butter in a
food processor. Strain and chill
until firm.*

*For Horseradish Butter, mix
2 teaspoons horseradish with
1/2 cup melted butter. Strain
and chill until firm.*

*Compound butters can
be stored, covered, in the
refrigerator for up to 3 months.*

Layered Summer Vegetables

*1 cup sliced yellow squash
1 cup sliced zucchini
1 1/2 cups shredded Cheddar cheese
1 large Vidalia onion, sliced
2 large tomatoes, sliced
butter
salt and pepper to taste
1/2 cup grated Parmesan cheese*

Alternate layers of the yellow squash, zucchini, half
the Cheddar cheese, onion and tomatoes in a baking dish,
beginning and ending with the yellow squash. Sprinkle with
the remaining Cheddar cheese and dot with butter. Sprinkle
with salt, pepper and Parmesan cheese.

Bake at 350 degrees for 30 to 40 minutes or until the
vegetables are cooked through.

Serves six

Lemon Parsley Butter

*Butter flavored with lemon and parsley is an easy
way to perk up potatoes, other vegetables, and even
broiled or grilled meats and fish.*

*1/2 cup (1 stick) unsalted butter, softened
1 to 2 teaspoons fresh lemon juice
1 tablespoon minced fresh parsley
1/2 teaspoon salt
1/2 teaspoon freshly ground pepper*

Cream the unsalted butter with the fresh lemon juice,
parsley, salt and pepper. Spread in a strip along the width of
a piece of waxed paper or parchment paper. Roll into a log,
using the waxed paper as a guide. Store in the refrigerator or
freezer for up to 3 months. Slice the chilled butter into
rounds to serve.

Makes one-half cup

Ratatouille

1 eggplant, peeled, chopped
1 large potato, peeled or unpeeled, chopped
1 zucchini, chopped
1 yellow squash, chopped
1 sweet onion, chopped
1 green bell pepper, chopped
1 red bell pepper, chopped
1 carrot, chopped
2 tablespoons chopped fresh parsley
$1/4$ cup olive oil
2 teaspoons Tabasco sauce
1 tablespoon salt
1 teaspoon pepper
4 tomatoes, chopped or sliced
$1/2$ cup uncooked rice
2 tablespoons wine vinegar
$1/4$ cup olive oil
$1/2$ cup water
2 cups shredded Monterey Jack cheese

Combine the eggplant, potato, zucchini, yellow squash, onion, bell peppers and carrot in a large bowl and mix well. Mix the parsley, $1/4$ cup olive oil, Tabasco sauce, salt and pepper in a small bowl. Pour over the vegetables and toss to coat well.

Arrange half the tomatoes in a greased 2-quart baking dish. Layer half the eggplant mixture over the tomatoes and sprinkle with the rice. Layer the remaining tomatoes and eggplant mixture over the rice.

Mix the vinegar, $1/4$ cup olive oil and water in a small bowl. Pour over the layers. Bake, covered, at 350 degrees for $1^1/2$ hours. Sprinkle with the cheese and bake, uncovered, for 30 minutes longer.

Do not use instant rice in this recipe.

Serves eight

Artichoke and Spinach Lasagna

The "oohs" and "ahs" received make this special lasagna well worth the time and effort.

Mornay Sauce
2/3 cup (1 1/3 sticks) unsalted butter
3/4 cup flour
5 cups milk
1 cup grated Parmesan cheese
salt and white pepper to taste

Artichoke Filling
2 (9-ounce) packages frozen artichoke
    hearts, thawed
6 ounces thinly sliced prosciutto
3 cups chopped leek bulbs
2 garlic cloves, minced
1/4 cup olive oil
1 tablespoon grated lemon zest
salt to taste

Lasagna
12 to 15 uncooked lasagna noodles
2 tablespoons salt
6 quarts water
1 pound ricotta cheese
1 cup grated Parmesan cheese
salt and white pepper to taste
6 ounces fresh spinach leaves
1 pound mozzarella cheese, shredded

For the sauce, melt the butter in a heavy large saucepan over medium heat. Stir in the flour and cook for 2 minutes or until bubbly and smooth, stirring constantly. Whisk in the milk gradually. Cook for 3 to 4 minutes or until thickened, whisking constantly. Add the Parmesan cheese gradually and cook until melted. Season with salt and white pepper. Remove from the heat.

For the filling, pat the artichoke hearts dry and cut into 1/2-inch strips. Cut the prosciutto into 1/2×3-inch strips. Sauté the leeks and garlic in the heated olive oil in a heavy large skillet over medium heat for 5 minutes or until tender but not brown. Add the artichoke hearts and prosciutto and sauté for 2 to 3 minutes longer, stirring frequently. Remove from the heat and stir in the lemon zest. Season with salt.

For the lasagna, cook the noodles with the salt in the water in a heavy large saucepan over high heat until the noodles are al dente. Drain and spread on kitchen towels. Combine the ricotta cheese with the Parmesan cheese in a bowl and mix well. Season with salt and white pepper.

Spread 1/3 of the sauce in a 10×14-inch baking pan and layer 1/3 of the noodles over the sauce. Layer half the spinach leaves and half the ricotta cheese mixture over the noodles and sprinkle with 1/3 of the mozzarella cheese. Layer half the artichoke filling and half the remaining noodles over the cheese.

Spread half the remaining sauce over the noodles and spread the remaining spinach leaves over the sauce. Layer the remaining ricotta cheese mixture, half the remaining mozzarella cheese and the remaining artichoke filling over the spinach. Top with the remaining noodles, sauce and mozzarella cheese.

Bake at 350 degrees for 45 to 50 minutes or until bubbly and light brown. Let stand for 10 to 15 minutes before serving.

You may prepare the lasagna in advance and store, covered, in the refrigerator for up to 1 day. Bring to room temperature before baking.

Serves twelve

Rigatoni with Broccoli and Gorgonzola

16 ounces uncooked rigatoni
salt to taste
6 cups broccoli florets
4 large garlic cloves, finely chopped
6 tablespoons olive oil
1 cup crumbled Gorgonzola cheese
pepper to taste

Cook the pasta in the salted water in a large saucepan for 8 minutes. Add the broccoli and bring back to a boil. Cook for 3 minutes or until the pasta is al dente and the broccoli is tender-crisp; drain and return to the saucepan.

Sauté the garlic in the heated olive oil in a heavy skillet. Add to the pasta in the saucepan and toss to coat well. Spoon into a serving bowl, sprinkle with the cheese and season with pepper. Toss again to serve.

Serves six

Chef Floyd Williams' Stuffed Tomatoes Italienne

Chef Floyd Williams plied his craft in the dining cars of the Norfolk and Western Railroad.

4 ounces spaghetti, broken, or macaroni
1 tablespoon salt
3 quarts water
6 large tomatoes
1 cup cooked ground beef
4 ounces mushrooms, sliced (optional)
1/2 cup shredded American cheese
1/3 teaspoon pepper
salt to taste

Cook the pasta with 1 tablespoon salt in the water in a large saucepan for 7 to 10 minutes or until tender; drain and rinse.

Scoop the pulp from the tomatoes, reserving the shells and the pulp of 4 tomatoes. Combine the reserved pulp with the ground beef, mushrooms, spaghetti and cheese in a bowl and mix well. Season with the pepper and salt to taste.

Spoon the mixture into the tomato shells and arrange in a greased baking dish. Bake at 350 degrees for 25 minutes.

Serves six

Dining Car Chefs

Dining car chefs were a talented and intrepid lot, creating the finest cuisine of their day in the swaying and cramped confines of a rail car. Their dishes were prepared from scratch without food processors, microwaves, or many of the gadgets that we take for granted today.

In the September 1947 issue of the Norfolk *and* Western Magazine, *John Jordan and Floyd Williams, two highly regarded rail chefs, included a few of their favorite recipes prepared for such patrons as the late President Franklin D. Roosevelt, who traveled to Roanoke via N&W in 1934.*

Harrison Hale, another prominent cook is long retired from the rails, but his beef tenderloin recipe is legendary in local culinary circles, and is still served to rave reviews.

Flavorful Rice Without the Fat

Rice is an easy and elegant side dish to complement an entrée. Cook it in chicken broth, beef broth, or beef consommé for an easy way to increase its flavor without adding a lot of fat or calories. Orange juice or apple juice will add the perfect flavor to rice that is to accompany chicken or pork.

Brown Rice

1 cup uncooked rice
1 (10-ounce) can beef consommé
1 (10-ounce) can beef bouillon
1/2 cup (1 stick) butter, melted
1 onion, finely chopped
1 (6-ounce) can chopped mushrooms, drained

Combine the rice, beef consommé, beef bouillon, butter, onion and mushrooms in a 2-quart baking dish and mix well. Bake at 375 degrees for 1 hour, stirring once or twice.

Serves six

Elegant Artichoke Rice

Add chopped cooked chicken for a great lunch or light supper.

1 cup uncooked rice
2 cups chicken broth
1 (12-ounce) jar marinated artichoke hearts
6 scallions, finely chopped
thyme to taste
1/4 teaspoon salt
1/3 cup mayonnaise
3/4 teaspoon curry powder

Cook the rice using the package directions, substituting the chicken broth for the water. Drain the artichokes, reserving 1/3 cup of the marinade. Add the artichokes, scallions, thyme and salt to the rice and mix gently.

Combine the reserved artichoke marinade with the mayonnaise and curry powder in a bowl and mix well. Add to the rice mixture and mix gently. Serve immediately or chill and serve as a salad.

Serves six to eight

Yellow Rice and Black Beans

1 (5-ounce) package saffron rice mix
1 (15-ounce) can black beans
2 tablespoons fresh lime juice
1 teaspoon chili powder
1/2 teaspoon cumin

Garnish
sour cream
sliced green onions
chopped fresh cilantro

Cook the rice mix using the package directions; keep warm. Drain the beans, reserving 1/4 cup liquid. Combine the beans, reserved liquid, lime juice, chili powder and cumin in a saucepan. Cook over medium heat until heated through.

Serve the beans over the rice. Garnish with sour cream, green onions and cilantro.
Serves three or four

Wild Rice and Spinach au Gratin

1 (5-ounce) package long grain and wild rice mix
1 (10-ounce) can beef broth
2 (10-ounce) packages frozen chopped spinach
8 ounces cream cheese, softened
salt to taste
16 ounces fresh mushrooms, thinly sliced
2 to 3 tablespoons butter

Cook the rice using the package directions and substituting the beef broth for an equivalent amount of the water called for. Cook the spinach using the package directions; drain. Add the cream cheese and salt and mix well. Sauté the mushrooms in the butter in a skillet just until golden brown.

Layer the rice, spinach mixture and mushrooms 1/2 at a time in a buttered 2-quart baking dish. Bake at 350 degrees for 40 minutes.
Serves six

Mushroom Risotto with White Wine

Wild mushrooms work well with this recipe, especially when served with game or red meat. It also makes a good vegetarian entrée.

1/2 cup chopped onion
2 tablespoons margarine or butter
1 cup dry white wine
2 cups uncooked arborio rice
3/4 teaspoon salt
pepper to taste
6 to 8 cups chicken broth
2 tablespoons margarine or butter
1 tablespoon olive oil
1/2 cup chopped onion
1 garlic clove, minced
8 ounces fresh mushrooms, thinly sliced
1 tablespoon minced fresh parsley
1 teaspoon dried thyme
1/4 teaspoon dried rosemary
1/4 teaspoon salt
1 cup grated Parmesan cheese

Cook 1/2 cup onion in 2 tablespoons margarine in a heavy saucepan over medium heat until tender. Add the wine and cook for 4 to 5 minutes or until the wine is reduced to 1/2 cup. Add the rice, 3/4 teaspoon salt and pepper to taste. Cook until the wine is absorbed, stirring constantly.

Heat the chicken broth in a large saucepan. Add the broth 1 cup at a time to the rice, cooking until the broth is absorbed after each addition and the rice is tender, a total of about 15 to 20 minutes, stirring constantly.

Melt 2 tablespoons margarine with the olive oil in a large skillet. Add 1/2 cup onion and garlic and sauté for 2 to 3 minutes or until the onion is tender. Add the mushrooms and sauté for 3 to 4 minutes or until the mushrooms are tender. Stir in the parsley, thyme, rosemary, 1/4 teaspoon salt and pepper to taste; keep warm.

Add the sautéed mushroom mixture and 1/2 cup of the Parmesan cheese. Serve with the remaining 1/2 cup Parmesan cheese.

Serves six

Sun-Dried Tomato Risotto

15 dry-pack sun-dried tomatoes
1 cup water
$2^1/2$ cups chicken broth or vegetable broth
$^1/2$ cup dry white wine
1 onion, finely chopped
1 garlic clove, minced
3 tablespoons olive oil
1 cup uncooked arborio rice
$^1/4$ to $^1/2$ cup grated Parmesan cheese
salt and pepper to taste

Garnish
chopped fresh parsley

Combine the sun-dried tomatoes with the water in a small saucepan and simmer for 1 minute; drain, reserving the liquid. Chop the tomatoes.

Combine the reserved tomato liquid, chicken broth and wine in a medium saucepan. Bring just to a simmer.

Sauté the onion and garlic in the olive oil in a large saucepan over medium-low heat until tender. Add the rice and sauté until the rice is coated well. Stir in the sun-dried tomatoes.

Add the heated broth mixture to the rice $^1/2$ cup at a time, cooking until the broth is absorbed after each addition and the rice is al dente, a total of about 17 minutes. Stir in the cheese, salt and pepper. Garnish with parsley.

Serves four to six

Dried Tomatoes

Prolong the enjoyment of your summer garden tomatoes by drying and storing them for a bleak February day. Simply cut large ripe tomatoes into $^1/4$-inch slices. Cut the slices into halves and arrange $^1/2$ inch apart on a foil-lined baking sheet. Place in a 150-degree oven with the door ajar and bake for 7 to 24 hours or until dry. Cool and place in containers with the date; store for up to 1 year.

Rise and Shine

Breads & Breakfast

Fincastle Bell-Ringing

While New York City might have Dick Clark and the Ball, and Roanoke might have its First Night celebration, Fincastle has its bells. For over three generations, this sleepy little town north of Roanoke has literally rung in the New Year.

Citizens bustle out from parties and gather in the heart of town at the Botetourt County Courthouse, although some townsfolk gather at and guard secret spots where the ambiance and acoustics reputedly cannot be matched.

The ceremony starts at 11:45 P.M. with the sounding of the courthouse bell. The bells of Fincastle Presbyterian Church, Fincastle Baptist Church, Fincastle United Methodist Church, and St. Mark's Episcopal Church are then rung consecutively until midnight. Taps is played, followed by three volleys from a shotgun. This truly lovely tradition climaxes with all bells ringing in unison for ten minutes.

Breads & Breakfast

Green Onion Biscuits

A delightful twist for a southern staple. These are wonderful the next day with another southern staple—ham.

3 cups flour
1 1/2 tablespoons baking powder
1 1/2 teaspoons salt
1 teaspoon freshly ground pepper
2 1/3 cups chilled heavy cream
1 1/2 cups thinly sliced green onions
2 tablespoons butter, melted

Mix the flour, baking powder, salt and pepper in a large bowl. Combine the cream and green onions in a medium bowl. Add to the dry ingredients and mix to form a dough.

Knead 8 times on a floured surface or just until smooth. Shape into an 8×8-inch square and cut into square 2×2-inch biscuits. Place 1 1/2 inches apart on a baking sheet and brush with the melted butter.

Bake at 425 degrees for 18 minutes or until golden brown. Serve warm. To rewarm biscuits, wrap in foil and heat in a 350-degree oven for 8 minutes.

Makes sixteen

Golden Cheddar Cheese Scones

4 cups flour
2 tablespoons baking powder
1/2 teaspoon baking soda
1/4 cup sugar
2 teaspoons salt
2 cups shredded Cheddar cheese
2 eggs
1 cup sour cream
1/2 cup vegetable oil
1/3 cup milk

Mix the flour, baking powder, baking soda, sugar and salt in a bowl. Stir in the cheese. Combine the eggs, sour cream, oil and milk in a medium bowl and mix well. Add to the cheese mixture and stir until moistened.

Knead 10 to 12 times on a floured surface. Roll 3/4 inch thick and cut with a 3-inch cutter. Place on a lightly greased baking sheet.

Bake at 400 degrees for 15 minutes. You may also drop the dough onto the baking sheet if preferred.

Makes one dozen

Festival in the Park

In June, when mornings are still cool and afternoons still bearable, Roanoke celebrates with an eleven-day spree of original art, jazz stylings, children's activities, sports, special attractions, and a rickety boat race down the Roanoke River.

Originally conceived and produced as an Arts Festival in 1969 by the League, Downtown Roanoke Association, and the Chamber of Commerce, it has blossomed into the region's largest community-wide celebration, and holds year-round events. Among other special events, Festival in the Park brings First Night Roanoke, a community New Year's Eve celebration; the International Wine Tasting Tour, and ShrimpFest to the community. Proceeds from the events provide scholarships to art students.

★ *Sidebar Stars*
Leslie and Chip Magee

Choosing Cornmeal

Cornmeal comes in either plain or self-rising forms and is ground from white, yellow, or blue corn. All three colors of cornmeal can be used interchangeably in recipes, but regular and self-rising cornmeal cannot be interchanged. Stone-ground cornmeal produces a bread with a coarser and slightly crunchier texture than regular cornmeal.

Corn Bread with Fresh Tomatoes and Mozzarella

4 ounces mozzarella cheese, cut into $^1/_2$-inch cubes
1 tablespoon unbleached flour
$^1/_2$ cup yellow cornmeal
$1^1/_2$ cups unbleached flour
2 tablespoons sugar
2 teaspoons baking powder
$^1/_2$ teaspoon baking soda
$^3/_4$ teaspoon salt
1 cup chilled buttermilk
2 eggs
$^1/_4$ cup olive oil
$^1/_4$ cup chopped fresh Italian flat-leaf parsley
$^2/_3$ cup chopped seeded Roma tomatoes

Toss the cheese with 1 tablespoon flour in a bowl to coat evenly. Combine the cornmeal, $1^1/_2$ cups flour, sugar, baking powder, baking soda and salt in a large bowl and whisk to mix well.

Combine the buttermilk, eggs, olive oil and parsley in a medium bowl and whisk to mix well. Add to the cornmeal mixture and stir just until moistened. Sprinkle the cheese and tomatoes over the batter and stir gently just until mixed.

Spoon into a buttered 9×9-inch baking pan. Place on a rack in the bottom third of an oven heated to 400 degrees. Bake for 22 minutes or until the top is golden brown and a tester inserted into the center comes out clean. Cool in the pan on a wire rack for 15 minutes. Cut into squares or wedges to serve.

Serves eight to ten

Blue Ribbon Corn Bread

1 1/2 cups stone-ground yellow cornmeal
1 2/3 cups sifted flour
2/3 cup sugar
1 tablespoon baking powder
1 teaspoon baking soda
1 1/2 teaspoons salt
1/2 cup (1 stick) butter, melted
1 1/2 cups buttermilk
1/2 cup milk
2 eggs, beaten
4 ounces warm corn kernels

Mix the cornmeal, flour, sugar, baking powder, baking soda and salt in a large bowl. Combine the butter, buttermilk, milk and eggs in a medium bowl and whisk until smooth. Add to the dry ingredients and mix just until moistened. Fold in the corn kernels; do not overmix.

Spoon into a buttered 7×9-inch baking dish. Bake at 425 degrees for 25 to 30 minutes or until the top is golden brown and a tester inserted into the center comes out clean.

Serves eight

Hotel Roanoke's Spoon Bread

1 1/2 cups cornmeal
1 teaspoon sugar
1 1/3 teaspoons salt
1 1/2 cups boiling water
1/4 cup (1/2 stick) butter, melted
5 eggs
2 cups milk
1 teaspoon baking powder

Mix the cornmeal, sugar and salt in a bowl. Add the boiling water and mix well. Stir in the butter. Beat the eggs with the milk in a bowl and add to the cornmeal mixture. Add the baking powder and mix well.

Spoon into a greased baking pan. Bake at 350 degrees for 30 to 40 minutes or until set.

Serves ten

Garden Week

The cheery yellow of forsythia signals the flowering of spring and is followed by the inimitable pastels of jonquils, tulips, daffodils, and hyacinths. Later come the blossoming pear, apple, and dogwood trees. Virginia is awash in color, and to celebrate, more than 40,000 tourists from all over the country descend upon Virginia annually for Historic Garden Week.

Conceived in 1929 as a means to raise funds for the restoration of the gardens of Virginia's many historic properties, member clubs of The Garden Club of Virginia, including the two Roanoke Clubs, open private and public houses and gardens from the Atlantic to the Appalachians.

The homes are grand, the gardens a riot of color, and the tour breathtaking, but, most importantly, in the seventy years since its inception, Garden Week has raised over five million dollars and the Garden Club has restored gardens at more than thirty-five historic properties.

★ *Sidebar Stars*

Mary Catherine and Duke Baldridge
Kelly and John Douthat
Gray and David Lawson
Martha and John Parrott

Heartland Bread Co.'s Blueberry Streusel Muffins

Muffins
2 cups unbleached flour
$^1/_2$ cup sugar
1 tablespoon baking powder
$^1/_4$ teaspoon baking soda
$^1/_2$ teaspoon salt
1 egg
$^1/_4$ cup ($^1/_2$ stick) butter, melted
$^1/_2$ cup milk
$^1/_2$ cup sour cream
1 teaspoon vanilla extract
$1^1/_2$ cups fresh blueberries

Streusel Topping
$^1/_2$ cup sugar
$^1/_3$ cup unbleached flour
$^1/_4$ cup ($^1/_2$ stick) butter, softened

For the muffins, mix the flour, sugar, baking powder, baking soda and salt in a large mixing bowl. Beat the egg in a medium bowl and add the butter, milk, sour cream and vanilla; mix well. Add to the flour mixture and stir just until moistened. Fold in the blueberries. Spoon into muffin cups sprayed with nonstick cooking spray, filling $^3/_4$ full.

For the topping, combine the sugar, flour and butter in a medium bowl and mix until crumbly. Sprinkle over the muffin batter.

Bake at 400 degrees for 18 to 20 minutes or until a wooden pick inserted into the center comes out clean.

Makes one dozen

Herbed Sour Cream Muffins

A savory alternative to traditional muffins.

2 1/4 cups unbleached flour
2 teaspoons baking powder
1/2 teaspoon baking soda
1 1/4 teaspoons salt
1 cup buttermilk
2 eggs
1/4 cup sour cream
2 tablespoons olive oil
1/4 cup chopped fresh chives
2 tablespoons chopped fresh basil
1 tablespoon chopped fresh dill
2 teaspoons chopped fresh marjoram
3/4 teaspoon grated lemon zest
melted butter

Combine the flour, baking powder, baking soda and salt in a large bowl and whisk to mix well. Combine the buttermilk, eggs, sour cream and olive oil in a medium bowl and whisk until smooth. Add the chives, basil, dill, marjoram and lemon zest and mix well. Add to the dry ingredients and mix until moistened.

Spoon into buttered or paper-lined muffin cups. Brush the batter lightly with melted butter. Place on the center rack of an oven heated to 350 degrees and bake for 20 minutes. Brush the tops again with butter and bake for 15 minutes longer or until a tester inserted into the center comes out clean. Remove the muffins and serve warm or cool on a wire rack.

Makes one dozen

Strawberries

When purchasing fresh strawberries, choose berries that are fully ripened with a deep red color and fresh-looking caps. Unlike many fruits, strawberries do not continue to ripen after being picked.

Strawberry Muffins

2 cups flour
2 teaspoons baking powder
salt to taste
$1/2$ cup (1 stick) unsalted butter, softened
$1^1/4$ cups sugar
2 eggs
$1/2$ cup half-and-half or cream
1 teaspoon vanilla extract
18 to 20 medium to large strawberries, chopped
$1/4$ cup sugar

Sift the flour, baking powder and salt together. Cream the butter and $1^1/4$ cups sugar in a mixing bowl until light and fluffy. Add the eggs 1 at a time, beating just until mixed after each addition. Add the dry ingredients alternately with the half-and-half, mixing until moistened. Add the vanilla and fold in the strawberries.

Spoon into greased muffin cups, filling nearly full. Sprinkle with $1/4$ cup sugar. Bake at 375 degrees for 30 minutes or until light brown. Remove to a wire rack to cool.
Makes fifteen

Chocolate Chip Banana Muffins

2 cups flour
1 teaspoon baking soda
$1/2$ teaspoon salt
$1/2$ cup (1 stick) butter, softened
1 cup sugar
2 eggs
1 teaspoon vanilla extract
3 ripe bananas, mashed
12 ounces (2 cups) chocolate chips

Mix the flour, baking soda and salt together. Cream the butter and sugar in a mixing bowl until light and fluffy. Beat in the eggs and vanilla. Add the bananas and mix well. Fold in the dry ingredients and chocolate chips.

Spoon into greased muffin cups. Bake at 350 degrees for 20 minutes or until golden brown.
Makes one dozen

Lemon Tea Bread

Bread
- 3/4 cup milk
- 1 tablespoon lemon juice
- 1 teaspoon thyme
- 2 cups flour
- 1 1/2 teaspoons baking powder
- 1/4 teaspoon salt
- 1/2 cup (1 stick) butter or margarine, softened
- 1 cup sugar
- 2 eggs
- 1 tablespoon grated lemon zest

Lemon Glaze
- 1 cup sifted confectioners' sugar
- 2 tablespoons lemon juice

For the bread, combine the milk, lemon juice and thyme in a saucepan and bring to a boil. Remove from the heat and let stand until cool. Mix the flour, baking powder and salt together in a bowl.

Cream the butter in a medium mixing bowl until light. Add the sugar gradually, beating until fluffy. Beat in the eggs 1 at a time. Add the dry ingredients alternately with the milk mixture, mixing well after each addition. Mix in the lemon zest. Spoon into a greased and floured 5×9-inch loaf pan. Bake at 325 degrees for 50 minutes or until a wooden pick inserted into the center comes out clean. Remove to a wire rack to cool.

For the glaze, mix the confectioners' sugar and lemon juice in a bowl until smooth. Drizzle over the cooled bread.

Makes one loaf

Pumpkin Apple Bread

Bread
- 3 cups flour
- 2 teaspoons baking soda
- 1 1/2 teaspoons cinnamon
- 1 teaspoon nutmeg
- 1/4 teaspoon allspice
- 3/4 teaspoon salt
- 1 (16-ounce) can pumpkin
- 3/4 cup vegetable oil
- 2 1/4 cups sugar
- 4 eggs
- 2 cups chopped peeled Granny Smith apples

Cinnamon Topping
- 1 tablespoon flour
- 5 tablespoons sugar
- 1 teaspoon cinnamon
- 1 tablespoon unsalted butter, softened

For the bread, sift the flour, baking soda, cinnamon, nutmeg, allspice and salt together. Combine the pumpkin, oil, sugar and eggs in a medium bowl and whisk until smooth. Add the dry ingredients and stir to mix well. Fold in the apples. Spoon into 2 buttered 5×9-inch loaf pans.

For the topping, combine the flour, sugar, cinnamon and butter in a bowl and mix until it resembles coarse meal. Sprinkle over the bread batter.

Place on the center rack of an oven preheated to 350 degrees. Bake for 50 minutes. Cool in the pans for 45 minutes. Remove to a wire rack to cool completely. Store, wrapped in plastic wrap, in the refrigerator for up to 1 week or in the freezer for up to 1 month.

Makes two loaves

Of Pots and Pipkins

In 1971, the League published its highly successful cookbook Of Pots and Pipkins. *A year later* Ladies Home Journal *featured the book and its creators at historic Cherry Hill Mansion. By 1982, more than 30,000 copies had been sold.*

Although no longer in print, Of Pots and Pipkins *endures. Its cuisine is the heart of southern cooking—fresh, nourishing, and lovingly prepared food for family and friends, whether by the handful or the hundreds. Those who own it, use it.* Oh My Stars! *continues this tradition by embracing its past and including particularly memorable recipes from* Of Pots and Pipkins. *They are indicated by a pipkin, and* *you are invited to continue to share them with your friends and family.*

Ethel Field's Hot Rolls

There is nothing more soul satisfying than hot breads, and these rolls are truly the best.

1 cup milk
$^1/_2$ cup (1 stick) butter
$^1/_2$ cup sugar
2 teaspoons salt
1 cake yeast
$^1/_4$ cup warm water
3 eggs
5 cups flour
melted butter

Bring the milk just to a simmer in a saucepan and add $^1/_2$ cup butter, sugar and salt; stir to mix well. Let stand until cool. Dissolve the yeast in the warm water.

Combine the eggs with the cooled milk mixture in a large bowl. Add the yeast mixture and mix well. Mix in the flour gradually. Knead until smooth on a floured surface. Place in a greased bowl, turning to coat the surface. Let rise in a warm place for 2 hours or until doubled in bulk.

Punch down the dough. Divide into smaller portions and roll 1 portion at a time on a floured surface. Cut with a round cutter. Score the circles in the center and dip half of each circle in melted butter. Fold the other half over the buttered half.

Arrange the rolls in a baking pan. Let rise in a warm place for 1 hour. Bake at 400 degrees for 8 minutes.

Makes six dozen

On the Rise Bread Company's Roanoke Star Bread

On the Rise is a destination for anyone in search of a good crusty European-style bread. The aroma of baking bread wafts onto Market Square enticing visitors and merchants alike.

1 teaspoon yeast
1 tablespoon salt
1¹/₂ cups cool water
3¹/₂ cups unnbleached flour

Dissolve the yeast and salt in the water in a bowl. Add the flour 1 cup at a time, mixing well after each addition; dough will be sticky. Knead on a floured surface for 10 minutes or until smooth.

Place in an ungreased bowl. Cover with plastic wrap and let rise for 3 hours. Punch down the dough and shape into a round loaf. Place on a baking sheet and let rise for 2 hours.

Cut a star shape on top of the loaf with a sharp knife. Bake at 400 degrees for 40 minutes or until the loaf sounds hollow when tapped on the bottom.

Makes one loaf

Commander's Garlic Bread

A treat from Commander's Palace Restaurant in New Orleans.

1 loaf French bread
2 garlic cloves, crushed
¹/₂ cup (1 stick) unsalted butter
¹/₄ cup chopped fresh dill
¹/₄ cup grated Parmesan cheese

Slice the bread into halves horizontally. Sauté the garlic in the butter in a small skillet for 2 minutes. Brush the butter mixture on the cut sides of the bread and sprinkle with the dill and cheese.

Place on a baking sheet and bake at 375 degrees for 5 to 8 minutes or until heated through. Cut crosswise into 1-inch slices. Serve immediately.

Serves six to eight

Blueberry Brunch Cake

Cake
- 2 cups fresh blueberries
- 3 cups flour
- 1 teaspoon baking powder
- 1/2 teaspoon baking soda
- 1/2 teaspoon salt
- 1/2 cup (1 stick) butter, softened
- 4 ounces cream cheese, softened
- 2 cups sugar
- 3 eggs
- 1 egg white
- 8 ounces lemon yogurt
- 2 teaspoons vanilla extract

Brunch Cake Glaze
- 1/2 cup confectioners' sugar
- 4 teaspoons lemon juice

For the cake, toss the blueberries with 2 tablespoons of the flour in a small bowl. Mix the remaining flour with the baking powder, baking soda and salt in a bowl.

Cream the butter, cream cheese and sugar in a mixing bowl at medium speed for 5 minutes or until light. Beat in the eggs and egg white 1 at a time. Add the flour mixture alternately with the yogurt, beginning and ending with the flour and mixing well after each addition. Fold in the blueberries and vanilla.

Spoon into a tube pan sprayed with nonstick cooking spray. Bake at 350 degrees for 1 hour and 10 minutes or until a wooden pick inserted in the center comes out clean. Cool in the pan for 10 minutes. Remove to a serving plate.

For the glaze, combine the confectioners' sugar and lemon juice in a bowl and mix until smooth. Drizzle over the warm cake.

You may substitute thawed frozen blueberries for the fresh blueberries if you prefer. Drain the berries well and pat dry.

Serves sixteen

Heartland Bread Co.'s Cinnamon Swirl Bread

Fabulous for French toast or just for snacking, this is a favorite with both adults and children.

2 envelopes dry yeast
1 1/2 cups warm (100-degree) water
1/4 cup honey
1 tablespoon salt
3 1/4 cups unbleached flour
3/4 cup honey
1/4 cup ground cinnamon

Dissolve the yeast in 1/2 cup of the warm water in a small bowl. Combine the remaining 1 cup warm water with 1/4 cup honey, salt and 2 1/2 cups of the flour in a large bowl and mix well by hand. Add the yeast mixture and mix to form a dough that pulls away from the side of the bowl. Add enough of the remaining flour to form a slightly dry dough.

Knead the dough on a lightly floured surface until firm and smooth. Return to the large bowl. Mix 3/4 cup honey with the cinnamon in a small bowl. Pour over the dough. Cover with a warm damp cloth and let rise in a warm place for 1 hour. Punch down gently and let rise, covered, for 1 hour longer.

Remove the dough carefully from the bowl without disturbing the honey and cinnamon mixture and place with the dry side down on a floured surface. Divide into 2 portions and roll the dough up to enclose the honey-cinnamon mixture pressing as much air out of the dough as possible.

Place the loaves seam side down into two 5×9-inch loaf pans. Let rise in a warm place for 20 to 30 minutes. Bake at 350 degrees for 30 to 35 minutes or until light brown. Remove to wire racks to cool.

Makes two loaves

The Proper Measure

To measure flour accurately, stir it lightly and spoon into a dry-ingredient measuring cup. Use the straight edge of a knife or spatula to level; avoid shaking the cup as this packs the flour.

Food Storage

Use milk within five days of the "sell by" date on the container.

Keep eggs no longer than four to five weeks in their original container in the refrigerator.

Store fresh or cooked poultry one or two days in the refrigerator or six months in the freezer.

Store beef, veal, or lamb roasts, steaks, or ribs for three to four days in the refrigerator or for up to six months in the freezer.

Cook fresh fish as soon as possible. Store cooked fish in the refrigerator for up to four days or in the freezer for up to six months.

Cook root vegetables such as potatoes, carrots, and turnips in seven to fourteen days. Serve broccoli, cauliflower, and Brussels sprouts in three to five days. Serve leafy or soft vegetables such as spinach or tomatoes in three to four days.

Classic Sour Cream Coffee Cake

2 cups unbleached flour
1 tablespoon baking powder
1/4 teaspoon salt
1 cup (2 sticks) unsalted butter, softened
2 cups sugar
2 eggs, beaten
1 cup sour cream
1 tablespoon vanilla extract
13/4 cups chopped pecans
3/4 cup sugar
1 tablespoon ground cinnamon

Sift the flour, baking powder and salt together. Cream the butter and 2 cups sugar in a mixing bowl until light and fluffy. Beat in the eggs. Add the sour cream and vanilla and mix well. Add the dry ingredients and mix just until moistened; do not overmix.

Combine the pecans with 3/4 cup sugar and the cinnamon in a medium bowl and mix well.

Layer the batter and the pecan mixture 1/2 at a time in a greased and lightly floured bundt pan. Place on the center rack of an oven heated to 350 degrees. Bake for 1 hour or until a tester inserted into the center comes out clean. Serve warm or at room temperature.

Serves ten

Orange Blossom French Toast

12 eggs
$1/2$ cup cream
2 tablespoons orange juice
grated zest of 1 orange
$1/2$ teaspoon vanilla extract
1 loaf French bread

Combine the eggs, cream, orange juice, orange zest and vanilla in a bowl and mix well. Pour into a shallow baking dish. Cut the bread into 1-inch slices and arrange in the dish, turning to coat well. Chill, covered, for 8 hours or longer.

Remove the bread slices to a greased baking sheet. Bake at 375 degrees for 20 to 25 minutes or until golden brown. Serve with maple syrup or fruit.

Serves six

Parkway Pancakes

For delightful apple pancakes, sift $1/2$ teaspoon cinnamon with the flour and add 1 cup of finely chopped peeled apples.

2 cups sifted flour
$3 1/2$ teaspoons baking powder
3 tablespoons sugar
1 teaspoon salt
1 egg
$1 3/4$ cups milk
3 tablespoons butter, melted, cooled

Sift the flour, baking powder, sugar and salt into a medium mixing bowl. Beat the egg with the milk in a small bowl. Add to the flour mixture and beat for 30 seconds or just until moistened, scraping down the side of the bowl. Stir in the butter.

Ladle onto a preheated griddle and cook until golden brown on both sides, turning once. Serve with syrup and butter or fruit.

Increase the milk to 2 cups for thinner pancakes.

Makes two dozen

Lower Fat Content

Replace mayonnaise or sour cream with plain nonfat or low-fat yogurt in salad dressings or other cold sauces to lower fat content.

Yogurt can also be used instead of cream in warm sauces if it is stirred in at the last minute and the mixture is not allowed to boil, which will curdle the yogurt.

To substitute yogurt in baking, substitute 1 cup of yogurt mixed with 2 tablespoons of cornstarch for 1 cup of cream.

Blueberry Gingerbread Pancakes

2 cups unbleached flour
1 1/2 teaspoons baking powder
1/4 teaspoon baking soda
1 1/4 teaspoons ground ginger
3/4 teaspoon pumpkin pie spice
1/4 teaspoon salt
3/4 cup light molasses
3/4 cup buttermilk
2 eggs
3 tablespoons vegetable oil
2 cups fresh or frozen blueberries

Sift the flour, baking powder, baking soda, ginger, pumpkin pie spice and salt twice. Combine the molasses, buttermilk, eggs and 3 tablespoons oil in a large bowl and whisk until smooth. Add the dry ingredients and mix well. Fold in the blueberries.

Heat a large nonstick skillet or griddle over medium-low heat and brush with oil for each batch of pancakes. Ladle 2 tablespoons of the batter onto the skillet for each pancake and spread into a 3-inch circle with the back of a spoon. Cook for 1 1/2 minutes on each side, turning once. Remove to a baking sheet and keep warm in a 200-degree oven for up to 20 minutes.

Makes sixteen

Sour Cream Waffles

1 cup flour, sifted
1 teaspoon baking powder
1 teaspoon baking soda
1 1/2 teaspoons sugar
1/8 teaspoon salt
3 egg yolks
2 cups sour cream
3 tablespoons butter, melted
3 egg whites

Sift the flour, baking powder, baking soda, sugar and salt into a large bowl. Beat the egg yolks in a medium bowl. Add the sour cream and butter and mix well. Add to the dry ingredients all at once and mix just until moistened. Beat the egg whites in a medium mixing bowl until stiff peaks form. Fold into the batter.

Spoon onto a heated waffle iron, using the manufacturer's instructions. Bake for 2 1/2 minutes or until no longer steaming. Serve with maple syrup.

Serves four to six

Corn Bread Crepes with Cheese and Roasted Peppers

This sophisticated dish works equally well for a light supper.

Crepes
3/4 cup cornmeal
3/4 cup flour
2 1/2 cups buttermilk
1/4 cup canola oil
4 eggs
1 teaspoon salt
1 cup coarsely chopped fresh or frozen corn kernels

Cheese and Roasted Pepper Filling
4 sweet onions
2 tablespoons butter
4 large red bell peppers, roasted (see page 25)
1 garlic clove, crushed
12 ounces goat cheese, crumbled
1/4 cup chopped fresh basil
freshly ground pepper to taste

Corn Sauce
2 cups coarsely chopped fresh or frozen corn kernels
2 cups heavy cream
salt to taste

Garnish
fresh basil sprigs

For the crepes, combine the cornmeal, flour, buttermilk, oil, eggs and salt in a blender container and process until smooth, scraping down the sides of the blender container once. Combine with the corn in a bowl and mix well. Chill for 1 hour.

Spray a nonstick 7-inch skillet with nonstick cooking spray and heat over medium heat. Add 1/4 cup of the batter at a time and tilt the pan to coat the bottom evenly. Cook for 3 minutes or until the top is set. Remove to waxed paper and repeat with the remaining batter.

For the filling, cut the onions into 1/4-inch slices and separate into rings. Sauté in the butter in a large heavy saucepan over medium-high heat for 20 to 25 minutes or until light brown. Remove and reserve 1 cup of the onions and 1/2 cup of the roasted peppers. Add the remaining roasted peppers to the onions. Add the garlic, cheese, basil and pepper and mix gently.

To fill and bake the crepes, spoon the cheese and pepper mixture onto the crepes and top with the reserved onions and peppers. Roll the crepes to enclose the filling and place seam side down in a 9×13-inch baking pan. Bake at 350 degrees for 15 to 20 minutes or until heated through.

For the sauce, combine the corn with the cream and salt in a small saucepan. Cook over low heat for 20 to 25 minutes or until thickened, stirring frequently. Serve over the crepes. Garnish with fresh basil.

Serves five

Asparagus and Basil Frittata

10 asparagus spears
salt to taste
10 eggs
$1/2$ cup grated Parmesan cheese
2 tablespoons sliced chives
$1/3$ cup chopped fresh basil
freshly ground pepper to taste
1 tablespoon olive oil

Trim the ends of the asparagus spears and cut into 1-inch pieces. Blanch in boiling salted water in a saucepan for 5 to 6 minutes; drain and immerse in ice water.

Combine the eggs, cheese, chives, basil, salt and pepper in a bowl and beat well. Heat the olive oil in a large skillet over medium-high heat. Spoon the egg mixture into the heated skillet and reduce the heat to medium. Cook until the edge of the egg mixture is set; do not stir. Add the asparagus and lift the edge of the eggs to allow the uncooked portion to reach the skillet. Cook until the center is set.

Place a large plate over the skillet and invert the frittata onto the plate. Slide the frittata back into the skillet and cook for 2 to 3 minutes longer. Broil just until the top is golden brown. Cut into wedges to serve.

For variety, add or substitute tomato sauce and Parmesan cheese; cooked fettucini with sautéed green onions and cooked shrimp; chopped ham and sautéed mushrooms; sautéed zucchini; or cooked sausage and bell pepper.

Serves eight

Cheese and Sausage Strata

8 ounces hot bulk pork sausage
8 slices bread, crusts removed, cut into $1/2$-inch cubes
12 ounces Monterey Jack cheese, shredded
4 eggs, lightly beaten
$1^1/2$ cups milk
1 teaspoon Dijon mustard
$1/2$ teaspoon Worcestershire sauce
$1/2$ teaspoon salt
cayenne pepper to taste
3 tablespoons butter, melted, cooled

Brown the sausage in a skillet over medium heat, stirring until crumbly. Remove the sausage with a slotted spoon to paper towels to drain. Brush a 1-quart soufflé dish with a small amount of the drippings from the skillet. Spread $1/3$ of the bread cubes in the prepared dish and sprinkle with $1/3$ of the cheese. Top with the sausage, the remaining bread cubes and $1/3$ of the cheese; press the layers lightly.

Combine the eggs, milk, Dijon mustard, Worcestershire sauce, salt and cayenne pepper in a bowl and whisk until smooth. Pour over the layers and top with the remaining cheese. Drizzle with the butter. Chill, covered, in the refrigerator for 1 to 24 hours. Bring to room temperature. Place dish in a larger pan and fill pan halfway up the sides with water. Bake at 350 degrees for 1 to $1^1/4$ hours or until golden brown and set.

Serves four

Garden Patch Strata

A lovely brunch idea, bursting with color and fresh flavor.

$^1/2$ cup chopped green onions
$^3/4$ cup chopped Vidalia onion
8 ounces fresh mushrooms, sliced
2 tablespoons olive oil
1 red bell pepper, cut into thin strips
1 green bell pepper, cut into thin strips
5 cups (1-inch) bread cubes
$1^1/2$ cups shredded sharp Cheddar cheese
$^1/2$ cup grated Parmesan cheese
6 eggs
$1^3/4$ cups milk
1 tablespoon Dijon mustard
$^1/4$ teaspoon Tabasco sauce
$^1/2$ teaspoon salt
$^1/2$ teaspoon pepper

Sauté the green onions, Vidalia onion and mushrooms in the olive oil in a skillet until tender. Add the bell peppers. Cook for 10 minutes or until the liquid evaporates, stirring frequently.

Layer the bread cubes, sautéed vegetables, Cheddar cheese and Parmesan cheese $^1/2$ at a time in a lightly greased 11×17-inch baking dish.

Combine the eggs, milk, Dijon mustard, Tabasco sauce, salt and pepper in a bowl and whisk until smooth. Pour over the layers. Chill, covered, for 8 hours. Let stand at room temperature for 15 minutes. Bake at 350 degrees for 45 minutes or until set.

Serves six

Egg Safety

Refrigerate eggs as soon as possible after purchase; store for up to five weeks after the packing date, which is a number stamped on the carton, with 1 representing January 1 and 365 representing December 31.

Keep eggs in the carton and store away from foods with strong odors.

Store separated eggs in airtight containers; whites will keep for one week and yolks for two days. Store hard-cooked eggs in their shells for up to one week.

Test for freshness by placing eggs in a container of water; fresh eggs will sink to the bottom.

Avoid recipes that use uncooked eggs, which are a hazard for salmonella bacteria. Discard cracked eggs, as salmonella bacteria can enter through cracks. Salmonella is most dangerous to the elderly, pregnant and nursing women, babies, and children.

Wash your hands before and after handling eggs.

Pepper Jack Cheese and Herb Soufflé

This is a crowd pleaser that can be prepared in advance.

1 pound pepper Jack cheese, cubed
3 ounces cream cheese, cubed
1 cup cottage cheese
2 tablespoons butter, chopped
8 eggs, lightly beaten
1 cup milk
¹/2 cup flour
1 tablespoon baking powder
herbs such as sage, dill, cilantro, thyme, rosemary and/or parsley to taste
salt and pepper to taste

Garnish
salsa

Combine the pepper Jack cheese, cream cheese, cottage cheese and butter in a bowl and toss to mix well. Spoon into a buttered 9×13-inch baking dish.

Combine the eggs, milk, flour, baking powder, herbs, salt and pepper in a bowl and mix until moistened. Pour over the cheese mixture.

Bake at 350 degrees for 40 to 45 minutes or until puffed and golden brown. Garnish with dollops of salsa.

You may prepare this and chill until baking time or bake in advance and microwave on High for 2 minutes to reheat.

Serves eight.

Cheddar Cheese Grits

1 cup quick-cooking grits
1 1/2 teaspoons salt
4 cups boiling water
6 tablespoons (3/4 stick) butter or margarine
1 1/2 teaspoons Worcestershire sauce
1 1/2 teaspoons hot pepper sauce
1 cup shredded sharp Cheddar cheese
1 tablespoon sherry
1 egg, beaten
1/2 cup shredded sharp Cheddar cheese

Stir the grits and salt into the boiling water in a saucepan. Cook, covered, over low heat for 5 minutes or until most of the water is absorbed. Remove from the heat and add the butter, Worcestershire sauce, hot sauce, 1 cup cheese and sherry. Stir until the cheese melts. Stir some of the hot mixture into the egg. Stir the egg mixture into the hot mixture.

Spoon into a greased 2 1/2-quart baking dish. Sprinkle with 1/2 cup cheese. Bake at 300 degrees for 1 hour or until bubbly.

You may prepare this 1 day in advance and store in the refrigerator. Bring to room temperature before baking.

Serves eight

About Grits

Grits are the ultimate southern comfort food, but they trace their origin back to the Algonquin who soaked dried corn in water and wood ashes to make tackummin or hummin, later Anglicized to hominy by the settlers.

Hominy could then be pounded into a coarse meal, boiled, and eaten hot as a cereal. In those first harsh New England winters, the Algonquin shared their hominy stores with the settlers to ward off their imminent starvation. Legend has it that one colonist declared it "equal to any bowl of groats she had ever tasted."

Some fifty years later, a Yankee ventured to Virginia with little more than a sack of the "groats" to his name. A Virginian agreed with the original colonists' assessment and declared them to be "good grits" and a southern staple star was born.

Adapted from Bert Greene's
The Grains Cookbook, *by Workman Publishing Company, Inc., 1988*

Starry Starry Delights

Desserts

Onward and Upward With the Arts

Roanoke is becoming a mecca for the performing arts. Opera Roanoke is one of the fastest-growing regional opera companies in America, featuring artists and directors from around the country. The company has received national bravos for its innovative approach to standard repertoire, as well as for baroque and modern opera.

Mill Mountain Theatre, a professional year-round theatre, is routinely praised as one of the best regional theatres in the country. The Theatre is committed to presenting new and original works, lavish musicals, gripping dramas, creative children's programs, and, of course, some old friends.

Roanoke is also home to a world-class symphony, whose productions are well subscribed and whose fund-raiser, Symphony Cup, brings polo to Roanoke. Hundreds annually venture to Green Hill Park to enjoy the last days of Indian summer, the polo match, and the sumptuous fare offered in the many private tents.

Valley Bank
Star Sponsor

Desserts

Chocolate Pâté with Raspberry Sauce

Pâté
    15 ounces semisweet chocolate
    1 cup heavy cream
    1/4 cup (1/2 stick) unsalted butter
    4 egg yolks
    3/4 cup confectioners' sugar
    6 tablespoons dark rum

Raspberry Sauce
    2 (10-ounce) packages frozen raspberries in syrup, thawed
    1/4 cup sugar
    3 tablespoons Grand Marnier

Garnish
    whipped cream

For the pâté, butter a 4-cup loaf pan and line it with waxed paper, leaving a short overhang; butter the waxed paper.

Combine the chocolate, cream and butter in a double boiler. Heat over simmering water until the chocolate and butter melt, whisking to blend well. Remove from the heat and beat in the egg yolks 1 at a time. Add the confectioners' sugar gradually, whisking constantly until smooth after each addition. Whisk in the rum. Spoon into the prepared pan. Cover with plastic wrap and freeze for 8 hours or longer.

For the sauce, drain the raspberries, reserving the juice from 1 package. Combine the raspberries, reserved juice, sugar and Grand Marnier in a food processor or blender container. Process until smooth. Strain into a bowl and chill until serving time.

To serve, remove the pâté gently from the pan; place the pan in hot water for several seconds if necessary to aid in removal. Invert onto a plate and remove the waxed paper. Cut into 1/3- to 1/2-inch slices with a hot knife. Spoon the raspberry sauce onto serving plates and place a slice of the pâté on each plate. Garnish with whipped cream.

Serves eight to ten

Cherry Hill

Over the years the League has had many homes, but none as lovely as Cherry Hill. Purchased jointly by the League and the Fine Arts Center in 1965, this stately 10-room modified Georgian home, flanked by three separate gardens, welcomed League members for eighteen years, and provided a gracious setting for an arts-hungry community. League-sponsored lecture series and lawn concerts and the Fine Arts Center's permanent collection, in addition to Cherry Hill's breathtaking teak floors, grand domed entrance hall, and sweeping staircases, drew crowds throughout the decades of the sixties and seventies. Although vacant for several years after its sale in 1983, it is now being restored to its former glory.

★ *Sidebar Stars*

Sharon Glaize "Spuzzie" Duckwall
Lucy Russell Ellett
Catherine Brownlee Smeltzer
Margaret Whitfield Wilks

Espresso Granita

The classic combination of coffee and dessert has been made trendy by street corner coffee shops. To increase its appeal in the sweltering humidity of a Virginia summer, combine the two into refreshing Espresso Granita. Combine 2 cups of hot regular or decaffeinated espresso with 1/4 cup sugar and 1 teaspoon coffee liqueur or coffee extract and stir to dissolve the sugar. Pour into a freezer-safe container and freeze for 20 minutes. Beat until smooth and return to the freezer. Repeat the process every 15 minutes until the mixture is the consistency of coarse sorbet. Serve in demitasse, topped with whipped cream and a coffee bean.

Frozen Chocolate Torte

A dessert that is both easy and beautiful and well worth the time required to prepare it.

Pecan Meringues
4 egg whites
1/2 teaspoon cream of tartar
1 cup sugar
3/4 cup chopped pecans

Chocolate Filling
2 cups whipping cream
3/4 cup chocolate syrup
1 teaspoon vanilla extract

Garnish
shaved chocolate
strawberries

For the meringues, draw two 8-inch circles on baking parchment or brown paper and place on a baking sheet. Beat the egg whites in a mixing bowl until frothy. Add the cream of tartar and beat until soft peaks form. Add the sugar 1 tablespoon at a time, beating constantly until stiff peaks form. Fold in the pecans.

Spoon into the circles on the baking parchment and spread with the back of a spoon. Bake at 275 degrees for 45 minutes. Turn off the oven and let the meringues stand in the closed oven for 45 minutes longer. Remove to a wire rack to cool.

For the filling, whip the cream in a mixing bowl until peaks form. Fold in the chocolate syrup and vanilla.

To assemble, spread the whipped cream over the tops of the meringues and stack on a serving plate. Freeze until firm. Let stand at room temperature for 30 minutes before serving. Garnish the top with shaved chocolate and arrange strawberries around the base.

Serves ten

Chocolate Hazelnut Truffle in Custard Sauce

In a word—decadent.

Truffle
1 cup heavy cream
1/4 cup (1/2 stick) butter
2 (8-ounce) bars semisweet chocolate, broken
4 egg yolks
3/4 cup confectioners' sugar
3 tablespoons Grand Marnier or orange juice
1 cup coarsely chopped hazelnuts, toasted

Custard Sauce
1/2 cup sugar
2 teaspoons cornstarch
6 egg yolks
2 cups heavy cream
2 teaspoons vanilla extract

For the truffle, line a 4×8-inch pan with foil, leaving a 1-inch overhang at each edge. Combine the cream, butter and chocolate in a heavy 2-quart saucepan. Cook over medium heat for 5 to 7 minutes or until the butter and chocolate melt, stirring to blend well. Remove from the heat and whisk in the egg yolks 1 at a time. Cook for 3 to 4 minutes or until the mixture reaches 160 degrees and thickens slightly, stirring constantly.

Remove from the heat and stir in the confectioners' sugar, Grand Marnier and hazelnuts. Pour into the prepared pan and freeze for 8 hours or longer.

For the custard, mix the sugar and cornstarch in a medium bowl. Add the egg yolks and whisk until light and smooth. Pour the cream into a saucepan and bring just to a boil over medium heat. Whisk a small amount of the hot cream into the egg yolk mixture; whisk the egg yolk mixture into the hot cream. Stir in the vanilla.

Cook over medium heat for 4 to 5 minutes or until the mixture reaches 160 degrees and is thick enough to coat the back of a metal spoon; do not boil. Pour into a bowl and chill in the refrigerator for 8 hours or longer.

To serve, lift the truffle from the pan using the foil and invert onto a plate; remove the foil. Cut into 16 slices with a hot knife. Spoon the custard onto serving plates and place a slice of the chocolate truffle on each plate.

Serves sixteen

Brown Bag It

It is common knowledge that placing fruit in a brown paper bag out of the direct sun will cause it to ripen. Few people realize, however, that adding a banana or apple to the bag will speed the process, as they emit a harmless gas that will ripen fruit faster.

Sliced Oranges with Grand Marnier

Fresh fruit marinated or macerated in wine, liqueur, or syrup is a light and elegant finish to an elaborate meal. The liquid and fruit can also be combined just at serving time for a quick dessert.

4 oranges
1 tablespoon sugar
1/4 cup Grand Marnier

Garnish
grated semisweet chocolate

Peel the oranges with a knife and separate into sections. Combine with the sugar and Grand Marnier in a bowl and mix gently. Marinate in the refrigerator for 8 hours or longer. Spoon into dessert cups or arrange on dessert plates to serve. Garnish with grated chocolate.
Serves four

For **Cantaloupe with Port,** cut cantaloupes into halves crosswise and pour 2 tablespoons of port into each half.

For **Peaches with Marsala,** peel and slice 4 ripe peaches and add 1/2 cup dry marsala and sugar to taste.

For **Plums in Red Wine,** cut 1 pound of plums into quarters and sprinkle with 2 to 3 tablespoons sugar. Add enough red wine to nearly cover and marinate for 1 hour.

For **Blueberries with Maple Cream,** wash and sort 1 pint of fresh or thawed and well-drained frozen blueberries. Combine with 1/4 cup maple syrup and marinate in the refrigerator for 1 hour or longer. Serve with a dollop of crème fraîche or sour cream and sprinkle with cinnamon.

JaMar Desserts' Peach Brandy Cheesecake

3 to 4 cups graham cracker crumbs
1/2 cup (1 stick) butter, melted
1 tablespoon small tapioca
2 tablespoons peach brandy
1 (16-ounce) package frozen sliced
    peaches, thawed

3 eggs, at room temperature
1 cup sugar
1/2 teaspoon nutmeg
24 ounces cream cheese, softened
16 ounces (2 cups) sour cream

Mix the graham cracker crumbs with the butter in a bowl. Press over the bottom and side of an 11-inch springform pan. Combine the tapioca, brandy and half the peaches in a small bowl and mix well. Marinate at room temperature for several minutes.

Combine the eggs, sugar and nutmeg in a food processor container and process until smooth. Add the cream cheese and sour cream and process to mix well.

Pour half the cream cheese mixture into the prepared springform pan. Top with the marinated peaches and the remaining cream cheese mixture. Bake at 300 degrees for 20 minutes. Reduce the oven temperature to 250 degrees and bake until set.

Cool on a wire rack and chill in the refrigerator for 2 hours. Place on a serving plate and remove the side of the pan. Top with the remaining peaches.

Serves fourteen to sixteen

Strawberry Cheesecake with Gingersnap Crust

Gingersnap Crust
3 cups crushed gingersnaps
1/4 cup sugar
1/4 cup (1/2 stick) unsalted butter,
    melted

Filling
24 ounces cream cheese, softened
3/4 cup sugar
1 teaspoon vanilla extract
3 eggs
2 cups fresh strawberry halves

For the crust, process the gingersnap crumbs, sugar and butter in a food processor until well mixed. Press over the bottom and halfway up the side of a 9-inch springform pan with a 2 1/2-inch side. Bake at 325 degrees on the center oven rack for 10 minutes. Cool on a wire rack.

For the filling, beat the cream cheese and sugar in a mixing bowl until light and fluffy. Add the vanilla and eggs and beat just until blended.

Spoon into the prepared crust. Bake at 325 degrees for 1 hour or until the side of the cheesecake is slightly puffed and begins to crack and the center is almost set when gently shaken.

Cool on a wire rack and chill, covered, for 8 hours or longer. Place on a serving plate and remove the side of the pan. Arrange the strawberries around the outer edge, Cut into wedges to serve.

Serves ten

159

Fresh Berry Cobbler

The best cobbler ever and so easy. You may substitute other berries or fresh fruit for the berries suggested.

2 cups fresh blackberries
2 cups fresh raspberries
1/4 cup sugar
1 cup flour
1/2 cup (1 stick) butter, melted
1 egg
1 cup sugar

Place the berries in a buttered 9-inch baking dish and sprinkle with 1/4 cup sugar. Combine the flour, butter, egg and 1 cup sugar in a bowl and mix well. Press over the fruit. Bake at 375 degrees for 45 to 60 minutes or until golden brown. Serve warm with whipped cream or French vanilla ice cream.

Serves eight

Strawberry and Rhubarb Crisp

Rhubarb is a favorite springtime treat, but this recipe works equally well with other seasonal fruits.

4 cups sliced fresh rhubarb
3 cups fresh strawberry halves
1 1/2 tablespoons cornstarch
1/2 cup sugar
6 tablespoons (3/4 stick) unsalted butter, softened
1 (7-ounce) package almond paste
1/3 cup sugar
1 cup flour

Toss the rhubarb and strawberries with the cornstarch and 1/2 cup sugar in a large bowl. Spoon into an 8-cup baking dish.

Process the butter, almond paste and 1/3 cup sugar in a food processor until blended. Combine with the flour in a medium bowl. Mix with fingers to form moist crumbs. Sprinkle over the fruit.

Bake at 400 degrees for 10 minutes. Reduce the oven temperature to 350 degrees and bake for 20 minutes longer or until the filling is bubbly and the topping is golden brown. Serve hot.

You may also prepare this in six 1 1/4-cup custard cups.

Serves six

The Greenbrier's Peach and Raspberry Torte with Almonds

Serve this versatile torte slightly warm with ice cream as a dessert, or sprinkled with confectioners' sugar as a breakfast treat.

1 cup flour
1¹/₂ teaspoons baking powder
¹/₂ teaspoon ground cinnamon
¹/₄ teaspoon ground nutmeg
¹/₂ teaspoon salt
²/₃ cup butter, softened
³/₄ cup sugar
1 egg
1¹/₄ cups finely ground blanched skinless almonds
4 canned or frozen peach halves, sliced
1 cup individually frozen raspberries without syrup, thawed

Butter the bottom and side of a 9-inch springform pan. Cover the bottom with a circle cut from baking parchment and butter the parchment.

Mix the flour, baking powder, cinnamon, nutmeg and salt together. Cream the butter in a mixing bowl until light. Add the sugar and cream for 1 or 2 minutes or until fluffy. Beat in the egg. Add the almonds and the dry ingredients and stir to mix well; batter will be stiff.

Spread half the batter in the prepared springform pan. Layer the peach slices and raspberries over the batter. Dollop the remaining batter over the top.

Bake at 350 degrees for 45 to 55 minutes or until the top is golden brown and the side pulls away from the pan. Cool on a wire rack for 5 to 10 minutes. Place on a serving plate and remove the side of the pan.

Serve twelve

The Greenbrier

The Greenbrier means many different things to the tens of thousands of guests who have stayed at America's Resort. Its archives trace its history from a frontier watering place to today's paradigm of grace and beauty. Throughout its illustrious 222-year history, world-class cuisine and elegant entertaining have been hallmarks of a unique brand of hospitality.

Not only does The Greenbrier excel in traditional cuisine, but it is also in the vanguard of new dishes and culinary techniques that are designed to appeal to ever-changing lifestyles.

Globally noted for its leadership in culinary education, The Greenbrier offers two-year apprentice programs for those seeking careers in the food arts. There is also an annual eight-week demonstration cooking school featuring some of the world's most distinguished chefs, cookbook authors, food writers, and restaurateurs. Add its seasonal daily gourmet cooking classes for both children and adults, and it's easy to understand why The Greenbrier has become the standard for professionals and amateur cooking aficionados alike.

Ikenberry Orchards

Billboards promising fresh cider and apples punctuate the countryside along Virginia Route 220, just northeast of Roanoke. A favorite stop is Ikenberry Orchards, which has been owned and operated by the Ikenberry family for almost a century.

Their retail market in a charming red frame building complete with front porch and rocking chairs is open year-round and offers locally grown apples, cider, peaches, and sweet corn in season. There is also a variety of homemade fruit preserves, apple butter, cured country hams, and brimming barrels of penny candy.

Ikenberry's is especially wonderful in the fall, when its orange-dotted hillsides are filled with children selecting their own great pumpkins, and picnic tables are filled with families enjoying a glorious day.

Virginia Apple Walnut Cake

4 large (about 2^1/$_2$ pounds)
    Granny Smith apples
^{1}/$_3$ cup honey
1 tablespoon ground cinnamon
3 cups flour
1 tablespoon baking powder
2 cups sugar
1 teaspoon salt
1 cup vegetable oil
4 eggs
^{1}/$_3$ cup orange juice
2 teaspoons vanilla extract
^{1}/$_2$ cup chopped walnuts
^{1}/$_2$ cup walnut halves

Line a 10-inch tube pan with baking parchment or coat with shortening or nonstick cooking spray. Peel the apples and slice ^{1}/$_4$ inch thick. Toss with the honey and cinnamon in a bowl.

Mix the flour, baking powder, sugar and salt in a mixing bowl. Add the oil, eggs, orange juice and vanilla and beat at low speed to mix. Beat at medium-high speed for 2 minutes or until smooth.

Spread ^{1}/$_3$ of the batter in the prepared tube pan. Drain the apples, reserving any juice. Arrange ^{1}/$_3$ of the apple slices in a spoke design over the batter and sprinkle with the chopped walnuts. Repeat the process to use the remaining ingredients.

Pour the reserved juices over the top and arrange the walnut halves around the outer edge. Place on a baking sheet with a rim. Bake at 350 degrees on the center oven rack for 1 hour and 20 minutes to 1^1/$_2$ hours or until a wooden pick or skewer inserted into the center comes out clean; cover loosely with foil if necessary to prevent overbrowning.

Cool in the pan for 10 minutes. Loosen the cake from the side of the pan with a knife and remove to a wire rack to cool completely. Loosen the cake from the tube and bottom of the pan with a knife and remove to a serving plate with a spatula.

Serves twelve to sixteen

Buttermilk-Glazed Carrot Cake

It is the buttermilk glaze that sets this apart from ordinary carrot cakes.

Cake
2 cups flour
2 teaspoons baking soda
2 teaspoons ground cinnamon
$1/2$ teaspoon salt
3 eggs
2 cups sugar
$3/4$ cup vegetable oil
$3/4$ cup buttermilk
2 teaspoons vanilla extract
2 cups grated carrots
1 (8-ounce) can crushed pineapple, drained
1 ($3^1/2$-ounce) can flaked coconut
1 cup chopped pecans or walnuts

Buttermilk Glaze
1 cup sugar
$1/2$ cup (1 stick) butter or margarine
1 tablespoon light corn syrup
$1/2$ cup buttermilk
$1^1/2$ teaspoons baking soda
1 teaspoon vanilla extract

Cream Cheese Frosting
$3/4$ cup ($1^1/2$ sticks) butter or margarine, softened
11 ounces cream cheese, softened
3 cups sifted confectioners' sugar
$1^1/2$ teaspoons vanilla extract

For the cake, line three 9-inch cake pans with waxed paper and lightly grease and flour the waxed paper. Mix the flour, baking soda, cinnamon and salt together.

Combine the eggs, sugar, oil, buttermilk and vanilla in a mixing bowl and beat until smooth. Add the dry ingredients gradually, mixing well after each addition. Fold in the carrots, pineapple, coconut and pecans.

Spoon into the prepared cake pans. Bake at 350 degrees for 25 to 30 minutes or until a wooden pick inserted into the center comes out clean.

For the glaze, combine the sugar, butter, corn syrup, buttermilk and baking soda in a saucepan and mix well. Bring to a boil over medium-high heat and boil for 4 minutes, stirring frequently. Remove from the heat and stir in the vanilla.

Drizzle the glaze over the hot cake layers. Cool the layers in the pans on a wire rack for 15 minutes. Remove to the wire rack to cool completely.

For the frosting, beat the butter and cream cheese at medium speed in a mixing bowl until light. Add the confectioners' sugar and vanilla and beat until smooth. Spread between the layers and over the top and side of the cake.

Serves sixteen

Chocolate Cake Decorations

Chocolate leaves, curls, or shells will turn an otherwise ordinary cake into a conversation piece and don't require a lot of time or effort. They can be made in advance and placed on or around the cake for a beautiful presentation.

To make Chocolate Leaves, you will need nontoxic leaves, such as rose leaves, that have not been treated with chemicals. Brush the underside of the leaves with melted chocolate and chill until firm. Pull the leaves away from the chocolate carefully.

To make Chocolate Curls, you will need a bar of good-quality chocolate at room temperature. Draw a vegetable peeler across the long side to create the curls.

To make Chocolate Shells, you will need two five-inch scallop shells. Cover the backs with plastic wrap and then with foil, molding tightly into the crevices of the shells. Brush the foil with oil and coat with melted chocolate and chill until firm. Separate the chocolate carefully from the shells and then from the foil.

The Best Chocolate Cakes

The addition of bourbon and strong coffee enliven these wonderful chocolate cakes.

4 ounces unsweetened chocolate, chopped
3 ounces bittersweet chocolate, chopped
3/4 cup (1 1/2 sticks) unsalted butter, sliced
1 1/2 cups brewed strong coffee
5 tablespoons bourbon
2 eggs, lightly beaten
1 teaspoon vanilla extract
2 cups flour
1 3/4 cups sugar
1 teaspoon baking soda
1/4 teaspoon salt

Garnish
whipped cream
raspberries

Butter two 7- or 8-inch springform pans and line the bottoms with waxed paper; butter and flour the waxed paper. Wrap the bottoms and 1 inch up the sides of the pans with foil to prevent leaks.

Melt the unsweetened chocolate, bittersweet chocolate and butter with the coffee in a 4-quart saucepan over medium-low heat, stirring to blend well. Cool for 10 minutes. Beat in the bourbon, eggs and vanilla. Add the flour, sugar, baking soda and salt and mix well; batter will be thin.

Spoon into the prepared springform pans. Bake at 275 degrees on the center oven rack for 1 to 1 1/4 hours or until a wooden pick inserted into the center comes out clean. Cool on wire racks.

Remove the sides of the pans and invert onto serving plates. Remove the pan bottoms and waxed paper. Garnish with whipped cream and raspberries.

Serves sixteen

Orange and Chocolate Roanoke Roulade

Cake Rolls
4 eggs
$^1/2$ cup water
1 (2-layer) package Swiss chocolate devil's food cake mix
$^1/4$ cup baking cocoa

Orange Cream Filling
2 cups whipping cream
5 to 6 tablespoons Grand Marnier
1 tablespoon finely grated orange zest
1 tablespoon baking cocoa

Orange and Chocolate Sauce
$^3/4$ cup half-and-half
12 ounces (2 cups) semisweet chocolate chips
$1^1/2$ cups miniature marshmallows
$^1/4$ teaspoon salt
$^1/4$ cup Grand Marnier

Garnish
orange zest curls

For the cake rolls, spray two 10×15-inch cake pans with nonstick cooking spray and line with waxed paper; spray the waxed paper.

Beat the eggs at medium-high speed in a large mixing bowl for 5 minutes. Add the water and beat at low speed to mix. Add the cake mix gradually, beating a low speed until moistened. Beat at medium-high speed for 2 minutes. Spread evenly into the prepared pans; layers will be thin.

Bake layers 1 at a time at 350 degrees on the center oven rack for 13 minutes or until the cake springs back when lightly touched in the center. Sift 2 tablespoons of the baking cocoa into a 10×15-inch rectangle on each of 2 smooth towels. Loosen the cakes from the pans and invert onto the baking cocoa. Roll up the cakes in the towels from the narrow sides. Place seam side down on wire racks and cool completely.

For the filling, beat the cream at medium-high speed in a mixing bowl until soft peaks form. Fold in 2 to 3 tablespoons of the Grand Marnier and the orange zest.

To fill, unroll the cakes and brush with the remaining Grand Marnier. Spread the filling over the cakes and reroll to enclose the filling. Dust with baking cocoa. Place seam side down on a plate and freeze, covered, for 1 hour or up to 3 months.

For the sauce, heat the half-and-half in a heavy saucepan over low heat. Stir in the chocolate chips, marshmallows and salt. Cook until the chocolate and marshmallows melt, stirring constantly. Remove from the heat and stir in the Grand Marnier. Cool to room temperature.

To serve, slice the cake rolls and place on serving plates. Top with the sauce and garnish with orange zest.

Serves twelve to sixteen

Coconut Oatmeal Cake

Cake
1¼ cups boiling water
1 cup rolled oats
1½ cups flour
1 teaspoon baking soda
1 teaspoon cinnamon
¼ teaspoon nutmeg
½ teaspoon salt
½ cup (1 stick) butter, softened
½ cup sugar
1 cup packed brown sugar
2 eggs, beaten
1 teaspoon vanilla extract

Walnut Topping
½ cup (1 stick) plus 2 tablespoons butter, softened
⅔ cup packed brown sugar
¼ cup light cream
⅔ cup chopped walnuts or pecans
1 cup packed shredded coconut

For the cake, pour the boiling water over the oats in a bowl and let stand for 20 minutes. Mix the flour, baking soda, cinnamon, nutmeg and salt together.

Cream the butter, sugar and brown sugar in a mixing bowl until light and fluffy. Beat in the eggs and vanilla. Add the oats mixture and mix well. Mix in the dry ingredients.

Spoon into a greased and lightly floured 9- or 10-inch springform pan. Bake at 350 degrees for 40 minutes. Cool on a wire rack.

For the topping, cream the butter in a mixing bowl until light. Add the brown sugar and beat until fluffy. Add the cream, walnuts and coconut and mix well.

Spread the topping over the cake. Broil just until golden brown. Cool on a wire rack. Place on a serving plate and remove the side of the pan.

Serves eight

Italian Cream Cake

Cake
2 cups flour
1 teaspoon baking soda
1/2 cup (1 stick) margarine, softened
1/2 cup shortening
2 cups sugar
5 egg yolks
1 cup buttermilk
1 teaspoon vanilla extract
1 (4-ounce) can flaked coconut
1 cup chopped pecans
5 egg whites

Cream Frosting
8 ounces cream cheese, softened
1/2 cup (1 stick) margarine, softened
1 (1-pound) package confectioners' sugar
1 teaspoon vanilla extract

Garnish
chopped pecans

For the cake, mix the flour and baking soda together. Cream the margarine and shortening in a mixing bowl until light. Add the sugar and beat until fluffy. Beat in the egg yolks. Add the flour mixture alternately with the buttermilk, mixing well after each addition. Stir in the vanilla, coconut and pecans. Beat the egg whites until stiff peaks form. Fold into the batter.

Spoon into 3 greased and floured 8-inch cake pans. Bake at 350 degrees for 25 minutes. Cool in the pans for 10 minutes. Remove to a wire rack to cool completely.

For the frosting, beat the cream cheese and margarine in a mixing bowl until smooth. Add the confectioners' sugar and beat until light. Beat in the vanilla.

Spread the frosting between the layers and over the top and side of the cake. Garnish with pecans.

Serves sixteen

The Icing on the Cake

For success frosting a cake, cool the cake layers completely and brush the crumbs from the tops and sides before spreading the frosting. Keep the cake plate tidy by placing several strips of waxed paper around the edges of the plate before stacking the layers and spreading the frosting; remove the strips before serving.

Test For Doneness

It isn't necessary to use a wooden pick to determine if a cake is done. First, the nose knows: when you begin to smell the wonderful aroma of the cake, it will be ready soon. Second, the eyes know: if the cake has begun to pull away from the side of the pan it is ready. Finally, the fingers know: lightly tap the center of the cake and if it springs back, it is time to take it out.

Frosted Brown Sugar Pound Cake

Cake
3 cups flour
$1/2$ teaspoon baking powder
1 teaspoon salt
$1^1/2$ cups (3 sticks) butter, softened
$3/4$ cup sugar
1 (1-pound) package brown sugar
5 eggs, at room temperature
1 cup evaporated milk
1 teaspoon vanilla extract

Brown Sugar Frosting
1 (1-pound) package brown sugar
$1/2$ cup evaporated milk
$1/2$ cup (1 stick) butter
1 teaspoon vanilla extract
$1/2$ teaspoon baking powder

For the cake, sift the flour, baking powder and salt together. Cream the butter, sugar and brown sugar in a mixing bowl until light and fluffy. Beat in the eggs 1 at a time. Add the sifted dry ingredients alternately with the evaporated milk, mixing well after each addition. Stir in the vanilla.

Spoon into a greased and floured 10-inch tube pan. Bake at 325 degrees for $1^1/4$ hours. Cool in the pan for 10 minutes. Remove to a wire rack to cool completely.

For the frosting, combine the brown sugar, evaporated milk and butter in a saucepan and bring to a boil. Cook for 3 minutes, stirring frequently. Remove from the heat and stir in the vanilla and baking powder. Place in a pan of ice water and beat until of spreading consistency.

To assemble, spread the frosting between the layers and over the top and side of the cake.

You may prepare this in 2 loaf pans if preferred and bake for 45 to 60 minutes or until the cakes test done.

Serves sixteen

Coconut Pound Cake

This cake freezes so well that it is actually better after being frozen.

1¹/2 cups (3 sticks) butter, softened
3 cups sugar
6 eggs, at room temperature
3 cups flour
¹/4 teaspoon baking soda
¹/4 teaspoon salt
1 cup sour cream, at room temperature
1 teaspoon vanilla extract
6 ounces flaked coconut

Cream the butter and sugar in a mixing bowl until light and fluffy. Beat in the eggs 1 at a time. Add the flour, baking soda, salt, sour cream and vanilla and mix well. Stir in the coconut.

Spoon into a greased and floured tube pan. Bake at 350 degrees for 1¹/4 hours. Cool in the pan for 10 minutes. Remove to a wire rack to cool completely.

Serves sixteen

Sour Cream Pound Cake

3 cups flour, sifted
¹/4 teaspoon baking soda
salt to taste
1 cup (2 sticks) butter, softened
3 cups sugar
6 eggs, at room temperature
1 cup sour cream, at room temperature
¹/2 teaspoon almond extract
1 teaspoon vanilla extract

Sift the flour, baking soda and salt together. Cream the butter in a large mixing bowl until light. Add the sugar gradually, beating constantly until fluffy. Beat in 2 of the eggs 1 at a time. Add the sour cream and mix well. Beat in the remaining 4 eggs 1 at a time.

Add the dry ingredients gradually, beating constantly until well mixed after each addition. Add the flavorings.

Spoon into a greased and floured tube pan. Bake at 325 degrees for 1¹/2 hours. Cool in the pan for 10 minutes. Remove to a wire rack to cool completely.

Serves sixteen

Fresh Apple Blondies

Fresh apples add a special touch to these treats! Serve them with vanilla ice cream and Butterscotch Sauce (page 171).

2 1/2 cups flour
2 teaspoons baking powder
1 teaspoon baking soda
1 teaspoon cinnamon
1 teaspoon salt
2 cups sugar

1 cup vegetable oil
2 eggs
2 teaspoons vanilla extract
3 cups chopped apples
1 cup chopped nuts (optional)
12 ounces (2 cups) butterscotch chips

Sift the flour, baking powder, baking soda, cinnamon and salt together. Combine the sugar and oil in a mixing bowl and beat until smooth. Add the eggs and beat until thickened. Add the dry ingredients and vanilla and mix well. Fold in the apples and nuts.

Spoon into a 9×13-inch baking pan sprayed with nonstick cooking spray. Sprinkle with the butterscotch chips and press the chips down lightly with a spatula. Bake at 350 degrees for 50 to 60 minutes or until a wooden pick inserted into the center comes out clean. Cool on a wire rack and cut into squares.

Serves fifteen

Triple-Chocolate Brownies

16 ounces (2 2/3 cups) semisweet
　　chocolate chips
6 ounces unsweetened chocolate
2 cups (4 sticks) unsalted butter
1 cup sifted flour
1 tablespoon baking powder
1 teaspoon salt
6 eggs

2 1/2 tablespoons instant espresso
　　granules
2 1/4 cups sugar
2 tablespoons vanilla extract
18 ounces (3 cups) semisweet chocolate
　　chips
3 cups chopped pecans or walnuts

Combine 16 ounces chocolate chips, unsweetened chocolate and butter in a double boiler. Melt over simmering water, stirring to blend well. Cool to room temperature.

Sift the flour, baking powder and salt together. Combine the eggs, espresso granules, sugar and vanilla in a bowl; do not mix. Add the chocolate mixture and stir to mix well. Add the sifted dry ingredients and mix well. Fold in 18 ounces chocolate chips and pecans.

Spoon into a greased and floured 12×18-inch baking pan. Bake at 350 degrees for 30 minutes or just until a wooden pick inserted into the center comes out clean; do not overbake. Cool on a wire rack and cut into squares.

Serves twenty

Clipper Chippers

These cookies were served at tea every afternoon on the "Nantucket Clipper."

2¹/₂ cups flour
1 teaspoon baking soda
¹/₂ teaspoon salt
1 cup (2 sticks) butter, softened
³/₄ cup sugar
³/₄ cup packed light brown sugar
1 tablespoon vanilla extract
1 tablespoon Frangelico
1 tablespoon Tia Maria
2 eggs
24 ounces (4 cups) milk chocolate chips
¹/₂ cup chopped pecans
¹/₂ cup chopped macadamias

Mix the flour, baking soda and salt together. Combine the butter, sugar, brown sugar, vanilla, Frangelico and Tia Maria in a mixing bowl and beat until light and fluffy. Beat in the eggs.

Add the dry ingredients gradually, mixing with a spoon. Fold in the chocolate chips, pecans and macadamias. Chill, covered, in the refrigerator for 8 hours or up to several days.

Drop by teaspoonfuls onto an ungreased cookie sheet. Bake at 325 degrees for 10 to 13 minutes or until golden brown. Cool slightly and serve warm.

The cookie dough may be frozen prior to baking. Refrigerating the dough enhances the flavors and helps the cookies keep their shape as they bake.

Makes five dozen

Butterscotch Sauce

Combine 2 cups packed brown sugar, ²/₃ cup light corn syrup and ¹/₄ cup butter in a saucepan and bring to a boil. Boil for 5 minutes and stir in ¹/₂ cup light cream and 1 teaspoon vanilla. Cool to room temperature and store in the refrigerator. Serve over ice cream, cake, or Fresh Apple Blondies (page 170).

Chocolate Toffee Cookies

Terrific served with ice cold milk.

1/2 cup flour
1 teaspoon baking powder
1/4 teaspoon salt
16 ounces bittersweet chocolate, chopped
1/4 cup (1/2 stick) unsalted butter
13/4 cups packed brown sugar
4 eggs
1 tablespoon vanilla extract
5 (11/4-ounce) chocolate-covered toffee bars, coarsely chopped
1 cup chopped toasted walnuts

Whisk the flour, baking powder and salt together in a small bowl. Combine the chocolate and butter in a double boiler. Melt over simmering water, stirring to blend well. Cool to lukewarm.

Combine the brown sugar and eggs in a mixing bowl and beat for 5 minutes or until thickened. Beat in the melted chocolate mixture and vanilla. Stir in the dry ingredients, chopped candy bars and walnuts. Chill in the refrigerator for 45 minutes or until firm.

Drop by 1/4 cupfuls 21/2 inches apart onto a parchment-lined cookie sheet. Bake at 350 degrees for 15 minutes or just until the tops are dry and cracked but the cookies are still soft to the touch. Cool on the cookie sheet. Store in an airtight container at room temperature for up to 2 days.

Makes eighteen

Pecan Crescents

A childhood holiday favorite that can be adapted to a low-sugar diet if not rolled in sugar. Do not substitute margarine for the butter.

1 cup (2 sticks) butter, softened
1/4 cup confectioners' sugar
1/2 teaspoon salt
2 cups flour
1 tablespoon vanilla extract
2 cups chopped pecans
2 to 3 cups confectioners' sugar

Cream the butter, 1/4 cup confectioners' sugar and salt in a mixing bowl until light and fluffy. Add the flour and mix well. Mix in the vanilla and pecans.

Shape into crescents and place on cookie sheets. Bake at 300 degrees for 10 to 12 minutes or just until they begin to brown. Remove from the cookie sheets and roll in additional confectioners' sugar.

Makes five dozen

Lemon Sandwich Cookies with Poppy Seeds

A perfectly exquisite tea cookie.

Cookies
2^3/4 cups flour
^{1}/2 teaspoon baking powder
^{1}/2 teaspoon salt
1 cup (2 sticks) unsalted butter, softened
1^1/4 cups sugar
1 egg
2 tablespoons poppy seeds
2^1/2 teaspoons grated lemon zest
1 teaspoon vanilla extract
^{1}/2 teaspoon lemon extract

Cream Cheese Filling
8 ounces cream cheese, softened
6^1/2 tablespoons sugar
^{1}/4 teaspoon vanilla extract
^{1}/2 teaspoon lemon extract

For the cookies, mix the flour, baking powder and salt together. Cream the butter in a large mixing bowl until light. Add the sugar gradually, beating constantly until fluffy. Beat in the egg, poppy seeds, lemon zest and flavorings. Add the dry ingredients gradually, mixing well after each addition.

Shape into a ball and divide into 2 portions. Flatten into disks and wrap in plastic wrap. Chill for 2 hours.

Roll 1 portion of the dough at a time ^{1}/8 inch thick on a floured surface. Cut with a fluted 2^1/2-inch cookie cutter. Arrange 1 inch apart on a buttered cookie sheet. Chill for 15 minutes.

Bake at 325 degrees for 18 minutes or just until the edges begin to brown. Cool on the cookie sheet for 3 minutes and remove to a wire rack to cool completely. Fill immediately or store in an airtight container at room temperature for up to 2 weeks or in the freezer for up to 1 month.

For the filling, combine the cream cheese, sugar and flavorings in a mixing bowl and beat until smooth.

To assemble, spread 2 teaspoons of the filling over the bottoms of half the cookies. Place the remaining cookies bottom down on the filling.

You may prepare these in advance and chill, covered, for up to 2 hours.

Makes two dozen

To Sift or Not to Sift

Flour is sifted during the milling process, so additional sifting is not necessary for most baked goods, although cake flour and all-purpose flour used for delicate cakes should be sifted to ensure that the texture of the cake is light and airy. It is also a good idea to stir the flour before measuring for any recipe because it tends to settle during shipping.

Mary Terry Goodwin Kuyk

Mary Terry Goodwin Kuyk, the League's founder and first president, was a woman noted for her humor, warmth, compassion, energy, and devotion to her family, friends, and community.

She was also known for her exquisite manners and impeccable style. In her day, she reigned as one of Roanoke's premier hostesses. Mrs. Kuyk remained active well into her nineties, addressing League meetings and attending the symphony and Garden Club functions.

She was, above all, a woman of extraordinary vision. Although born to a life of privilege, she viewed voluntarism as rent to be paid for her place in the community. Of her many achievements, she was proudest of the League-sponsored scholarship awarded each year in her name to high school students who enriched the community through their volunteer efforts.

Praline Cookies

You may have some of the topping left over to serve on vanilla ice cream. It can also be stored in the freezer until needed.

Cookies
1 cup (2 sticks) butter, softened
1 cup confectioners' sugar
2 cups flour
1 cup chopped pecans
1 tablespoon vanilla extract

Praline Topping
$^1/_2$ cup (1 stick) butter
1 cup packed brown sugar
$^1/_4$ teaspoon salt
$^1/_2$ cup evaporated milk
2 cups confectioners' sugar
$^1/_2$ teaspoon vanilla extract

For the cookies, cream the butter and confectioners' sugar in a mixing bowl until light and fluffy. Add the flour, pecans and vanilla and mix well.

Shape into 1-inch balls and place on an ungreased cookie sheet. Make an indentation in each ball with the thumb or the end of a wooden spoon. Bake at 375 degrees for 15 to 17 minutes or just until the edges are very light brown. Remove to a wire rack to cool.

For the topping, melt the butter in a saucepan. Add the brown sugar and salt and bring to a boil. Cook for 2 minutes, stirring constantly. Remove from the heat and stir in the evaporated milk. Bring to a boil and cook for 2 minutes longer. Remove from the heat and stir in the confectioners' sugar and vanilla. Spoon into the wells in the cookies and let stand for 20 to 30 minutes or until set.

Makes two dozen

Seven-Layer Squares

¹/₂ cup (1 stick) butter
1 cup graham cracker crumbs
1 cup flaked coconut
6 ounces (1 cup) chocolate chips
6 ounces (1 cup) butterscotch chips
1 (14-ounce) can sweetened condensed milk
1 cup chopped pecans

Melt the butter in a 9×13-inch baking dish. Press the graham cracker crumbs into the butter. Layer the coconut, chocolate chips and butterscotch chips over the crumb layer. Drizzle evenly with the sweetened condensed milk and sprinkle with the pecans.

Bake at 350 degrees for 25 to 30 minutes or until golden brown. Cool in the pan. Chill in the refrigerator and cut into squares.

Makes two dozen

Chocolate Chip Pecan Pie

2 eggs
¹/₂ cup sugar
¹/₂ cup packed brown sugar
¹/₂ cup flour
¹/₂ cup (1 stick) butter, melted, cooled
1 teaspoon vanilla extract
1 cup broken pecans
6 ounces (1 cup) semisweet chocolate chips
1 unbaked (9-inch) pie shell

Beat the eggs lightly in a mixing bowl. Add the sugar and brown sugar and beat until smooth. Add the flour, butter and vanilla and mix well. Stir in the pecans and chocolate chips.

Spoon into the pie shell. Bake at 350 degrees for 1 hour. Cool on a wire rack.

Serves six to eight

Food Safety for Picnics

Summer is for picnics, but you should take precautions against food poisoning, even in vegetable- and fruit-based dishes, which scientists have recently discovered may also harbor harmful bacteria. To keep salads worry-free:

Refrigerate fruits and vegetables at 40 degrees or lower for 8 hours or longer before preparing the dish.

Rinse whole fruits and vegetables in cold running water before slicing, packing, or serving them. In most cases, the only place that bacteria can live is on the surface of the food, unless it has been cut and mixed into the dish.

Wash your hands before cutting vegetables and fruits and use a clean knife and nonporous cutting board.

Use a well-insulated cooler with an ice pack, and keep it in the shade with the top closed.

Streusel-Topped Peach Pie

Pastry
1 1/2 cups flour
2 teaspoons sugar
1/2 cup vegetable oil
1 teaspoon salt
2 tablespoons milk

Peach Filling
4 cups (or more) sliced fresh peaches
1/2 cup confectioners' sugar
1/3 cup flour

Streusel Topping
3/4 cup flour
3/4 cup packed light brown sugar
1 teaspoon cinnamon
6 tablespoons (3/4 stick) unsalted butter, slightly softened

For the pastry, mix the flour and sugar in a bowl. Add the oil, salt and milk and mix to form a soft dough. Press into a 9-inch pie plate and flute the edge.

For the filling, combine the peaches with the confectioners' sugar and flour in a bowl and mix gently. Spoon into the pie shell.

For the topping, combine the flour, brown sugar, cinnamon and butter in a bowl and mix with a pastry blender until crumbly. Sprinkle over the pie.

Bake at 375 degrees for 40 to 50 minutes or until the topping is golden brown. Cool on a wire rack.

Serves eight

Crème de Menthe Ice Cream Pie

Pie
2 cups chocolate wafer crumbs
$1/3$ cup butter, melted
3 pints vanilla ice cream
5 tablespoons crème de menthe

Chocolate Topping
3 ounces unsweetened chocolate
$1/2$ cup water
$3/4$ cup sugar
$1/4$ teaspoon salt
$4^1/2$ tablespoons butter
$3/4$ teaspoon vanilla extract

For the pie, mix the chocolate wafer crumbs with the melted butter in a bowl. Press into a 10-inch pie plate. Chill for 1 hour.

Soften the ice cream in a large bowl. Drizzle the crème de menthe over the ice cream and swirl to marbleize. Spoon into the chilled pie shell. Freeze until firm.

For the topping, melt the chocolate with the water in a saucepan over low heat, stirring to blend well. Add the sugar and salt. Cook for 5 minutes or until the sugar dissolves and the mixture thickens, stirring constantly. Remove from the heat and add the butter and vanilla. Cool to room temperature.

Spread the topping evenly over the pie. Freeze, covered, until firm.

Serves eight

Lemon Ice Cream Pie

Arrange sliced fresh strawberries around the edge for a special presentation.

$1^1/2$ cups graham cracker crumbs
6 tablespoons ($3/4$ stick) butter, melted
$1/4$ cup sugar
$1/2$ gallon French vanilla ice cream
1 (12-ounce) can frozen lemonade concentrate, thawed

Garnish
mint sprigs

Mix the graham cracker crumbs, butter and sugar in a bowl. Press firmly into a 9-inch pie plate.

Soften the ice cream in a mixing bowl and add the lemonade concentrate; beat to blend well. Spoon into the prepared pie plate. Cover with foil and freeze for 8 hours or longer. Garnish servings with mint.

Serves eight

Twinkle Twinkle

Kid Stuff

Little Chefs

I will make you brooches and toys for your delight,
Of birdsong at morning and starshine at night.
Robert Louis Stevenson
"Songs of Travel," The Vagabond

Like the vagabond, children have an uncanny, if occasionally frustrating, ability to conjure up magical and fanciful creations from both the most elusive and the most ordinary of ingredients. With a little ingenuity and patience, however, adults can turn the culinary portion of this knack into a lifelong celebration of good nutrition and a love affair with cooking.

Children, with a little supervision, can measure, mix, stir, and knead. Their assistance is invaluable in cutting out and later decorating holiday cookies. They can set the table, rinse dishes, and, eventually, make their own lunches.

The kitchen acts as teacher as well. In measuring, children learn the practical applications of fractions. In following recipes, children learn the importance of following directions. Cooking, like making toys from starshine, is alchemy, so let the little chefs go. Let them enjoy the kitchen as you do.

Kid Stuff

Activities

Chicken Noodle Soup

1 (3 1/2-pound) chicken
16 cups canned reduced-sodium chicken broth
1/2 cup chopped onion
2 carrots, peeled, thinly sliced
2 ribs celery, sliced
1 cup sliced mushrooms
2 tablespoons butter
1 tablespoon fresh lemon juice
8 ounces uncooked wide egg noodles
1/2 cup finely chopped fresh parsley
salt and pepper to taste

Cut the chicken into 8 pieces. Combine with the chicken broth in a heavy large saucepan and bring to a boil. Reduce the heat and simmer, loosely covered, for 20 minutes or until the chicken is tender. Remove the chicken with tongs, reserving the broth. Cool the chicken and cut into bite-size pieces, discarding the skin and bones.

Skim the fat from the chicken broth and bring to a simmer. Add the onion, carrots and celery. Simmer for 8 minutes or until the vegetables are tender.

Sauté the mushrooms in the butter in a heavy large skillet over medium-high heat for 5 minutes. Stir in the lemon juice. Add to the vegetable mixture in the chicken broth. Add the noodles, parsley and chicken. Simmer for 5 minutes or until the noodles are tender. Season with salt and pepper.

Serves twelve

The Arts Council of the Blue Ridge

Serving as a major voice and advocate for cultural groups and individual artists in the region, The Arts Council provides services, a resource library, and an on-line artist registry. Regular programs include the Roanoke City Art Show, the Laban Johnson Arts Scholarship, Art in the Window, the Arts and Cultural Educational Directory, *the Real Art/Real Cheap Sale, and a regional quarterly newsletter.*

Strawberry Pretzel Salad

2^1/2 cups crushed pretzels
3 tablespoons sugar
^{3}/4 cup (1^1/2 sticks) butter, melted
8 ounces cream cheese, softened
1 cup sugar
2 cups whipped topping
2 (3-ounce) packages strawberry gelatin
2 cups boiling water
2 (10-ounce) packages frozen strawberries

Mix the crushed pretzels, 3 tablespoons sugar and melted butter in a bowl. Press over the bottom of a 9×13-inch baking dish. Bake at 350 degrees for 10 minutes. Cool to room temperature.

Beat the cream cheese and 1 cup sugar in a mixing bowl until smooth. Add the whipped topping and mix well. Spread over the cooled pretzel layer.

Dissolve the gelatin in the boiling water in a bowl. Add the strawberries and mix gently. Spoon over the cream cheese layer. Chill until firm.

Serves ten to twelve

Favorite Mac and Cheese

Superlative! The easiest, cheesiest, creamiest version of this classic you will find.

16 ounces uncooked smooth or ridged elbow macaroni
1 tablespoon vegetable oil
^{1}/2 cup shredded Muenster cheese
^{1}/2 cup shredded sharp Cheddar cheese
^{1}/2 cup shredded mild Cheddar cheese
^{1}/2 cup shredded Monterey Jack cheese
^{1}/2 cup cubed Velveeta cheese
^{1}/2 cup (1 stick) butter
2 eggs, lightly beaten
2 cups half-and-half
coating mix for oven-fried chicken

Cook the macaroni using the package directions and adding the oil to the cooking water. Drain the macaroni and return it to the saucepan. Reserve 2 tablespoons of each of the cheeses to top the macaroni. Add the remaining cheeses and butter to the macaroni in the saucepan. Cook over low heat until the cheeses and butter melt, stirring constantly. Add the eggs and half-and-half and mix well.

Spoon into a large baking dish and sprinkle with the reserved cheeses. Top with the coating mix. Bake at 350 degrees for 30 minutes.

Serves four to six

Banana Pops

6 large firm bananas
12 popsicle sticks or skewers
12 ounces semisweet or milk chocolate, broken
chocolate sprinkles, frosting and/or assorted candies for
  decoration

Cut each banana into halves crosswise. Insert a wooden popsicle stick or skewer 2 inches or more into each banana half. Place on a foil-lined tray and freeze for 1 hour or until firm.

Melt the chocolate in a heavy saucepan over low heat. Spoon the chocolate over the bananas 1 at a time, coating evenly. Decorate with chocolate sprinkles, frosting and/or candies.

Arrange gently on a waxed-paper lined tray or insert the sticks into florist's foam to hold upright. Wrap lightly with foil and freeze until serving time. Serve frozen.

Serves twelve

Doughnuts

2 (10-count) cans refrigerator biscuits
1/4 cup (about) jam or jelly
vegetable oil for frying
superfine sugar for coating

Separate the biscuit dough into individual biscuits and press on waxed paper to flatten. Spoon about 1 teaspoon of the jam into the center of 10 of the biscuits. Top with the remaining biscuits and press the edges to seal.

Pour enough oil into a skillet or electric skillet to fill halfway. Heat the oil to 380 degrees. Add the doughnuts. Fry until golden brown on both sides, turning once. Drain on paper towels and roll in sugar.

Makes ten

Happiness

Mix 2 heaping measures of patience with 1 heart full of love, 2 handfuls of generosity and a head full of understanding. Add a dash of laughter and sprinkle generously with kindness. Mix well with plenty of faith. Spread over a lifetime and serve up to everyone you meet!

Dirt Cake

1 new clay flowerpot
1/4 cup (1/2 stick) margarine, softened
8 ounces cream cheese, softened
1 cup confectioners' sugar
3 1/2 cups milk
2 (4-ounce) packages French vanilla instant pudding mix
12 ounces whipped topping
1 large package chocolate sandwich cookies, crushed
1 silk flower
12 gummy worms
12 small garden trowels

Wash the flowerpot and line it with foil. Beat the margarine, cream cheese and confectioners' sugar in a mixing bowl until light and fluffy. Combine the milk, pudding mix and whipped topping in a bowl and beat until smooth. Add the cream cheese mixture and mix well.

Alternate layers of the cookie crumbs and pudding mixture in the prepared flowerpot until all ingredients are used, ending with the cookie crumbs. Chill, covered, for 8 to 12 hours before serving.

To serve, insert a silk flower into the "dirt" and arrange gummy worms around the flowers. Serve with a small garden trowel as a spoon.

Serves twelve

Flowerpot Baked Alaskas

An elegant treat for a teddy bear picnic.

10 next-to-smallest-size clay flowerpots
8 egg whites
1 1/4 cups sugar
1 angel food or pound cake
12 drinking straws
1/2 gallon ice cream
10 flowers
10 mint leaves

Wash the flowerpots in the dishwasher and cool. Beat the egg whites in a mixing bowl until frothy. Add the sugar gradually, beating until stiff peaks form.

Slice the cake and place 1 slice in the bottom of each flowerpot. Hold a straw upright in the center of each flowerpot and fill the flowerpot 3/4 full with ice cream, packing around the straw. Cut off the straw even with the top of the flowerpot. Spread the meringue around the straw. Freeze until serving time.

Bake the desserts at 400 degrees just until the meringue is golden brown. Insert the flower into each straw and decorate with mint leaves.

Serves ten

Awesome Gingerbread

1 1/3 cups flour
1/2 teaspoon baking powder
1/2 teaspoon baking soda
3/4 teaspoon cinnamon
3/4 teaspoon ginger
1/2 teaspoon allspice
1/2 teaspoon salt
1/2 cup shortening
1/2 cup packed brown sugar
1/2 cup boiling water
1/2 cup molasses
1 egg, lightly beaten
3/4 cup raisins (optional)
Lemon Sauce (below)

Mix the flour, baking powder, baking soda, cinnamon, ginger, allspice and salt in a large mixing bowl. Combine the shortening, brown sugar, boiling water and molasses in a bowl and mix until smooth. Mix in the egg. Add to the dry ingredients and beat until smooth. Stir in the raisins.

Spoon into an 8- or 9-inch baking pan with a greased bottom. Bake at 350 degrees for 30 to 40 minutes or until the gingerbread tests done. Serve with Lemon Sauce.

Serves nine

Lemon Sauce

A southern classic that is great on gingerbread.

1/4 cup (1/2 stick) margarine, softened
1 cup sugar
1 egg, beaten
2 tablespoons lemon juice
1 teaspoon grated lemon zest
1/3 cup boiling water

Cream the margarine and sugar in a mixing bowl until light and fluffy. Add the egg, lemon juice and lemon zest and mix well. Mix in the boiling water.

Spoon into a saucepan and bring just to a boil over medium heat, stirring constantly. Remove from the heat and cool. Store in the refrigerator. Reheat to serve.

Makes one cup

Juicing Citrus Fruits

To yield the maximum amount of juice from a lime, lemon, or orange, first roll it on a hard surface. Then submerge it in hot water for 15 minutes or pierce it and microwave for 30 seconds before squeezing.

Cone Creations

Cones are not just for ice cream anymore. To transform an ordinary pantry item into something magical, try these suggestions:

For a gruesome witch, perch a chocolate cone on a frosted chocolate cupcake, decorate with green gummy eyes, a candy corn nose, and jagged miniature marshmallow teeth.

For a harvest tepee, remove the tip of the cone. Invert the cone and attach 3 pretzel sticks to the top with frosting. Pipe orange, brown, and black native American designs on the side.

For a festive Christmas tree, cover an inverted cone with green frosting and decorate with candy-coated chocolates, gum drops, jelly beans, or whatever captures your fancy. Top, of course, with a star.

Cupcake Cones

1 (2-layer) package favorite cake mix
12 flat-bottom ice cream cones
1 (16-ounce) can favorite prepared frosting
sprinkles, miniature chocolate chips and/or small candies

Prepare the cake mix using the package directions. Spoon it into the ice cream cones and place on a baking sheet. Bake until a wooden pick inserted into the cake comes out clean. Cool on a wire rack.

Spread with the frosting and decorate with sprinkles, chocolate chips or candies.

Makes one dozen

Pumpkin Patch Pie

Puts the treat in Trick or Treat.

1 pint orange sherbet
12 ounces whipped topping
1 chocolate sandwich cookie pie shell
9 chocolate sandwich cookies, crushed

Soften the sherbet slightly in a bowl and stir until smooth. Add half the whipped topping and mix well. Spoon into the pie shell and sprinkle with the crushed cookies; press the crushed cookies into the sherbet mixture. Top with the remaining whipped topping. Freeze for 4 hours or until firm.

Serves eight

Kids' Sushi

8 favorite flavor roll-up fruit snacks
3 tablespoons butter
3 cups miniature marshmallows
3 cups crisp rice cereal
16 gummy worms

Unroll the fruit snacks and arrange plastic sheet side down on a work surface. Melt the butter in a 3-quart saucepan over low heat. Add the marshmallows and cook until the marshmallows melt, stirring constantly with a wooden spoon to blend well. Stir in the cereal.

Spread $^1/_2$ cup of the mixture quickly over each fruit snack, leaving a 1-inch edge at the top. Place 2 gummy worms side by side along the bottom edge. Roll the fruit snacks tightly to enclose the filling, peeling off the plastic sheets as you roll. Press the top borders to seal. Cut each roll into 4 pieces.

Makes thirty-two

Old-Fashioned Rock Candy

3 cups favorite fruit juice
6 cups sugar
$^3/_4$ teaspoon cream of tartar
flavoring extract to complement juice chosen
food coloring (optional)

Combine the fruit juice, sugar and cream of tartar in a heavy saucepan and mix well. Cook to 290 degrees on a candy thermometer, soft-crack stage; do not stir. Remove from the heat and add the flavoring and food coloring. Pour into a layer $^1/_4$ inch deep in a greased square pan. Chill until firm. Invert the pan to remove the candy and break into pieces.

You may also pour the mixture into a $^1/_4$-inch layer in greased individual molds and chill until firm.

Serves twelve

Peanut Butter and Jelly Candy

Children love to make these!

1 cup peanut butter
1 cup favorite-flavor jelly
1 cup powdered milk granules
graham cracker crumbs or chopped nuts

Combine the peanut butter, jelly and milk granules in a bowl and mix well. Shape into small balls and roll in the graham cracker crumbs. Chill until serving time.
Makes two dozen

Superballs

1 cup (2 sticks) margarine, melted
8 ounces graham crackers, crushed
1 (12-ounce) jar peanut butter
1 cup chopped pecans
1 cup flaked coconut
12 ounces (2 cups) chocolate chips
1/2 bar paraffin

Combine the margarine, graham cracker crumbs, peanut butter, pecans and coconut in a bowl and mix well. Shape into balls.

Melt the chocolate chips with the paraffin in a saucepan, stirring to blend well. Dip the balls into the chocolate mixture using wooden picks and place on waxed paper. Let stand until cool and firm.
Makes two dozen

Egg Nest Treats

Top off an Easter egg hunt with these adorable treats.

6 ounces (1 cup) semisweet chocolate chips
6 ounces (1 cup) butterscotch chips
1 (5-ounce) can chow mein noodles
jelly beans

Mix the chocolate chips and butterscotch chips in a microwave-safe dish. Microwave on High until the chips melt; stir until smooth. Stir in the noodles.

Drop by teaspoonfuls onto waxed paper and shape into nests with the back of a spoon. Fill with jelly beans and let stand until set.

Makes two dozen

Peanut Haystacks

A favorite autumn and Halloween treat.

1 tablespoon smooth peanut butter
6 ounces (1 cup) butterscotch chips
1 cup roasted peanuts
1 (3-ounce) can chow mein noodles

Melt the peanut butter and butterscotch chips in a heavy saucepan over low heat, stirring to blend well. Stir in the peanuts and noodles. Drop onto waxed paper. Chill until firm.

Makes two dozen

Homemade Baby Food

An infant's first solid food needn't come from a box or jar. To ensure the freshest ingredients for your baby, select your own produce and microwave, steam, or boil it until tender. Mash it with a fork or purée to the desired consistency in a blender or food processor, adding liquid if needed. Store in airtight containers in the refrigerator or freeze in ice cube trays.

Yummies

1 cup sugar
1 cup light corn syrup
1 cup chunky peanut butter
6 cups Special K cereal
6 ounces (1 cup) butterscotch chips
6 ounces (1 cup) chocolate chips

Combine the sugar and corn syrup in a large saucepan. Bring to a rolling boil over medium heat, stirring occasionally. Stir in the peanut butter. Pour over the cereal in a bowl and mix well. Press onto a buttered large cookie sheet.

Melt the butterscotch chips and chocolate chips in a heavy saucepan over low heat, stirring to blend well. Spread over the cereal mixture. Cut into squares while warm. Let stand until cool.
Makes forty

Monster Cookies

Something for everyone!

6 eggs
1 cup (2 sticks) margarine, softened
1¹/2 cups packed brown sugar
1¹/2 cups sugar
2 tablespoons vanilla extract
24 ounces peanut butter
4 teaspoons baking soda
9 cups rolled oats
8 ounces "M & M's" Chocolate Candies
8 ounces (1¹/3 cups) chocolate chips

Beat the eggs in a mixing bowl. Add the margarine and beat until smooth. Add the brown sugar, sugar, vanilla, peanut butter and baking soda in the order listed, mixing well after each addition. Stir in the oats, candies and chocolate chips.

Drop by teaspoonfuls onto a cookie sheet. Bake at 350 degrees for 13 minutes. Cool on the cookie sheet for several minutes. Remove to a wire rack to cool completely.

You may also scoop the batter onto the cookie sheet by ¹/2 cupfuls for monster Monster Cookies.
Makes six dozen

Reese's Cup Cookies

36 miniature Reese's Cup candies
1/2 cup (1 stick) butter, softened
1/3 cup peanut butter
1/2 cup sugar
1/2 cup packed brown sugar
1 egg
1 teaspoon vanilla extract
1 3/4 cups flour
1 teaspoon baking soda
1/2 teaspoon salt

Remove the wrappers from the candies. Cream the butter, peanut butter, sugar and brown sugar in a mixing bowl until light and fluffy. Beat in the egg and vanilla. Add the flour, baking soda and salt gradually, mixing well after each addition.

Spoon the batter into greased miniature muffin cups, filling 1/2 to 2/3 full. Bake at 375 degrees for 8 to 9 minutes or until the cookies test done. Place 1 candy in the center of each cookie immediately and let stand in the muffin cups for 10 minutes.

Twist the cookies in the muffin cups gently to loosen. Chill in the refrigerator or let stand for 20 minutes longer or until firm. Remove from the muffin cups.

Makes three dozen

Scotcheroos

1 cup sugar
1 cup corn syrup
1 cup peanut butter
6 cups crisp rice cereal
6 ounces (1 cup) chocolate chips
6 ounces (1 cup) butterscotch chips

Mix the sugar and corn syrup in a 3-quart saucepan. Cook over medium heat until bubbly, stirring frequently. Remove from the heat and stir in the peanut butter. Add the cereal and mix well. Press into a buttered 9×13-inch dish.

Melt the chocolate chips and butterscotch chips in a heavy saucepan over low heat, stirring to blend well. Spread over the cereal layer. Cool completely. Cut into squares.

Makes two dozen

Scratch and Sniff Watercolors

Beat the summer doldrums or rainy-day blues with this boredom blaster. Mix 1 tablespoon powdered drink mix with 1 tablespoon warm water in a small container. Repeat the process to create as many color/flavors as desired. Use the mixtures to paint a fruit basket. Allow the painting to dry for 8 hours or longer. Scratch the paint and sniff. You may not create a masterpiece, but the grapes will smell like grapes and the oranges will smell like oranges.

Christmas Sugar Cookies

This dough will keep in the refrigerator for a week, ready to bake fresh cookies every day during the holiday season.

4 to 5 cups flour
1 teaspoon baking soda
2 teaspoons cream of tartar
1/2 teaspoon ground nutmeg
1 teaspoon salt
1 cup (2 sticks) butter, softened
2 1/4 cups sugar
3 medium eggs, beaten
1 teaspoon lemon juice
1 teaspoon vanilla extract

Mix the flour, baking soda, cream of tartar, nutmeg and salt together. Cream the butter and sugar in a mixing bowl until light and fluffy. Beat in the eggs, lemon juice and vanilla. Add the dry ingredients and mix to form a dough.

Place in a sealable plastic bag and chill for several hours or up to a week. Roll a small amount of the dough at a time 1/4 inch thick on a floured surface. Cut with a cookie cutter and place on a greased cookie sheet.

Bake at 350 degrees for 10 minutes or just until the cookies begin to brown. Cool on the cookie sheet for several minutes. Remove to a wire rack to cool completely. Decorate or frost as desired.

Makes five dozen

Cookie Cutter Sugar Cookies

2 1/2 cups flour
1 teaspoon baking soda
1 teaspoon cream of tartar
1 cup (2 sticks) butter, softened
1 1/2 cups confectioners' sugar
1 egg
1 teaspoon vanilla extract
1/2 teaspoon almond extract

Mix the flour, baking soda and cream of tartar together. Cream the butter and confectioners' sugar in a mixing bowl until light and fluffy. Beat in the egg and flavorings. Add the dry ingredients and mix to form a dough. Chill for 2 hours or longer.

Roll the dough on a floured surface and cut with a cookie cutter. Place on a cookie sheet. Bake at 375 degrees for 7 to 8 minutes or until light golden brown. Cool on the cookie sheet for several minutes. Remove to a wire rack to cool completely.

Makes three dozen

Homemade Lemonade

Sugar Syrup
  4 cups sugar
  4 cups water

Lemonade
  fresh lemon juice
  water
  lemon slices

For the sugar syrup, combine the sugar and water in a saucepan and cook until the sugar dissolves. Bring to a boil and remove from the heat. Store in the refrigerator until needed for lemonade.
  To make lemonade, combine 1 part of the sugar syrup mixture with 1 part lemon juice in a pitcher. Add 3 parts water and mix well. Chill until serving time. Serve over ice and add fresh lemon slices.
  Makes thirty-six servings

Purple Cows

  2 cups milk
  2 cups vanilla ice cream
  1 (6-ounce) can frozen grape juice concentrate

  Combine the milk, ice cream and grape juice concentrate in a blender container and process until smooth. Serve in glasses.
  Serves four

Recipe for Children's Needs

- *Affection in equal share for all your children*

- *Relationships that are close*

- *Welcome for their friends in your home*

- *Peace maintained in front of them*

- *Thoughtfulness for everyone in the family*

- *Truthfulness; never lie to children*

- *Answers for all their questions*

- *Discipline that is consistent; never punish them in the presence of others*

- *Constancy in affection and moods*

- *Validation of their good points rather than concentration on their failings*

- *Serves everyone*

Shirley Temples

Great fun for a special occasion or birthday party.

1 (8- to 10-ounce) jar maraschino cherries with stems
2 (1-liter) bottles ginger ale, chilled
8 orange slices

Drain the cherries, reserving the juice. Pour 2 tablespoons of the juice over ice in each glass and add 2 cherries. Fill the glasses with ginger ale and add an orange slice.
Serves eight

Big Lick Superbubbles

Make this recipe in quantities, pour into a backyard wading pool, and invite the neighborhood for an afternoon of summer fun. Big wands and even kitchen funnels make enormous bubbles.

1/4 cup clear liquid dishwashing soap
1/4 cup (or more) glycerine
3/4 cup water
1 tablespoon sugar
bubble wands

Combine the dishwashing soap, glycerine, water and sugar in a bowl and mix well. Dip the wands into the mixture to blow bubbles.
The glycerine is available at most drug stores.
Makes one and one-fourth cups

Fruity Lip Gloss

Little girl heaven.

2 tablespoons shortening
1 tablespoon favorite-flavor powdered drink mix
1 (35-millimeter) plastic film container

Combine the shortening and drink mix in a small microwave-safe dish. Microwave on High for 30 seconds or until the shortening melts; stir to mix well. Pour into the film container and chill for 20 to 30 minutes or until firm.
Makes one

Puddin' Paint

1 (4-ounce) package vanilla instant pudding mix
2 cups very cold water
food coloring

Combine the pudding mix and water in a bowl and whisk for 2 minutes or until smooth. Chill in the refrigerator for 5 minutes. Spoon the pudding mixture into small bowls and add 5 to 7 drops of different food coloring to each bowl; mix well. Paint pictures and lick fingers at will.
Makes two cups

Clean Hands in a Twinkle

Research shows that more than 90 percent of germs can be eliminated by washing hands in warm soapy water for 15 seconds, or the time it takes to sing the well-known first verse of "Twinkle, Twinkle Little Star." For tougher jobs, additional verses might be needed:

Twinkle, twinkle, little star
How I wonder what you are!
Up above the world so high,
Like a diamond in the sky.

Twinkle, twinkle, little star
How I wonder what you are!

When the blazing sun is gone,
When he nothing shines upon,
Then you show your little light,
Twinkle, twinkle, all the night.

Then the traveller in the dark,
Thanks you for your tiny
*   spark,*
He would not know which
*   way to go,*
If you did not twinkle so.

In the dark blue sky you keep,
And often through my
*   curtains peep,*
For you never shut your eyes,
'Til the sun is in the sky.

Twinkle, twinkle, little star
How I wonder what you are!

Baker's Clay

4 cups flour
1 cup salt
1 1/2 cups cold water
drinking straw
paint

Combine the flour and salt in a bowl. Add the water and mix until smooth. Knead by hand or in a food processor for 10 minutes. Place in a sealable plastic bag and let rest for 12 to 24 hours before using. Store in the refrigerator or freezer.

Shape the clay by hand or roll on a work surface and cut as desired. Press a straw through the dough while it is still soft for items to be hung. Place on a cookie sheet and let stand until dry. Paint as desired.

You may also dry the clay items in a 200- to 225-degree oven for 2 to 3 hours if preferred.

Makes five cups

Oatmeal Play Clay

1/2 cup (or more) flour
1/2 cup water
1 cup rolled oats
6 to 8 drops of food coloring

Combine 1/2 cup flour, water, oats and food coloring in a medium bowl and mix well. Add additional flour if the mixture is too sticky. Knead on a floured surface for 3 to 4 minutes. Store in an airtight container in the refrigerator.

Makes two cups

Play Dough I

2 cups water
1/2 cup salt
food coloring
2 tablespoons vegetable oil
2 cups flour
2 tablespoons alum

Bring the water to a boil in a saucepan and add the salt, stirring to dissolve the salt completely. Remove from the heat and add the food coloring, vegetable oil, flour and alum; mix until smooth.

Place in a plastic bag and cover with a towel; knead until the dough is smooth and evenly colored. Store in an airtight container.

You can find the alum in the spice section of most grocery stores.

Makes four cups

Play Dough II

2 cups water
2/3 cup salt
2 tablespoons vegetable oil
4 teaspoons cream of tartar
2 packages powdered drink mix
2 cups flour

Combine the water, salt, oil, cream of tartar and drink mix in a saucepan and mix well. Bring just to a simmer and remove from the heat; do not boil. Add the flour and mix to form a dough. Knead until smooth. Store in an airtight container.

Do not use lemonade drink mix for this recipe. You may substitute food coloring for the drink mix if you prefer.

Makes four cups

Good Clean Fun

With just a little guidance kids can make their own fanciful soap. All it takes is an ice cube tray, petroleum jelly, food coloring, and a bar of glycerine from the drugstore. Brush a small amount of the food coloring on the bottom of a microwave-safe bowl and add the glycerine to the bowl. Microwave on High until the glycerine melts, stirring frequently to blend well and color evenly. Coat the ice cube tray with petroleum jelly and pour in the glycerine mixture, filling almost to the top. Cool for several hours or until firm. Pop the soap out of the trays and wash up for dinner!

A Starry Salute

Oh My Stars! would not have been possible without the support of the many, many people and organizations that offered their financial support, time, and energy to make this book come to life. We offer our heartfelt thanks for those immeasurable gifts.

We salute The Rutherfoord Companies for their three-year financial commitment to the book.

For their corporate financial assistance, we salute the following companies:

Advance Auto Parts
Elaine Stephenson Interiors, Inc.
James River Equipment Company
Next Day Gourmet
Provisions Gourmet
R. R. Donnelly and Sons
Roanoke Electric Steel Corporation
Valley Bank
Valley Investors Corporation

For their personal financial contributions, we salute the following individuals:

Susan and Jim Bailey
Mary Catherine and Duke Baldridge
Nancy O. Barbour
Mikki and Stephen Barranco
Jennifer B. Baucom
Katherine C. Bezold
Barbara S. "Bobbie" Black
Madeline A. Bounds
Betty Tom A. Bradshaw
Trudy and Robert Brailsford
Susan H. Bray
Adrienne G. Bullington
Helen A. Burnett
Nancy K. Carson
Regina G. Carson
Sandra G. Carson
Mary Elizabeth R. "Mimi" Coles
Julie B. Comer
Paige Comer
Jane E. Coulter
Wendy C. Cummings
Laura M. Davis
Mary R. Delaney
Christine H. Douthat

Kelly S. Douthat
Sharon G. "Spuzzie" Duckwall
Mollie W. Elder
Lucy R. Ellett
Kelly and Russ Ellis
Sibyl N. Fishburn
Cristina B. Flippen
Janet and Jim Frantz
Jan B. Garrett
Clydenne R. Glenn
Melissa S. Godsey
Eva D. Goldsmith
Mary F. Green
Harriet S. Heinemann
Diane and Steven Higgs
Virginia B. "Ginny" Jarrett
Linda S. Kaufman
Kay J. Kelly
Mary Elizabeth Y. Kepley
Doris C. Kreger
Ruth Ellen D. Kuhnel
Jennifer W. Landry
Gray L. Lawson
Nancy H. Leggett

Betty H. Lesko
Ann S. Levan
Ona M. Litwiller
Leslie and Chip Magee
Kathryn Manning
Julia H. Murden
Teresa A. Nowak
Kathleen K. Oddo
Betty Brooke M. Parrott
Martha F. Parrott
Anne Marie S. Poore
Stewart Putney
Nancy B. Robertson
Susanne O. Roderick
Lorie K. Rogers
Diane M. Rosenberg
Lauren D. Saunders

Virginia T. Shackelford
Chera L. Sink
Catherine B. Smeltzer
Mary Stuart C. Stanley
Elaine E. Stephenson
Ann K. Stevens
Katharine D. Stevens
Barbara B. Stockstill
Shannon H. Summerlin
Nicole B. Terrill
Shari B. Thomas
Tracey Thompson
Dolly F. Wallenborn
Laura Ann Whitlow
Margaret W. Wilks
Lee H. Woody
Sandra S. Worthy

For delving into their trove of Roanoke's favorite recipes,
we salute the following restaurants:

Alexander's
105 South Jefferson Street
540-982-6983

Angler's Cafe
310 Second Street
540-342-2436

Billy's Ritz
102 Salem Avenue
540-342-3937

Café Succotash
210 South Pollard Street
540-981-2100

Corned Beef and Co.
Restaurant, Bar, and Billiards
107 South Jefferson Street
540-342-3354

The Greenbrier
White Sulphur Springs, WV
304-536-1110

Heartland Bread Co.
Towers Shopping Center
540-342-7323

The Homestead
Hot Springs, VA
800-838-1766

Hotel Roanoke and Conference Center
110 Shenandoah Avenue
540-985-5900

Hunting Hills Country Club
5220 Hunting Hills Drive
540-774-4427

JaMar Desserts
411 South Jefferson Street
540-342-0159

Lib Wilhelm Catering
604 Fifth Street
540-344-1317

Montano's International Gourmet
3733 Franklin Road
540-344-8960

On The Rise Bread Company
303 Market Street
540-344-7715

Stephen's Restaurant
2926 Franklin Road
540-344-7203

Wertz's Country Store and
Wine Cellar, Inc.
215 Market Street
540-342-5133

A Starry Salute

For sharing their time-tested recipes, new classics and most dearly held secrets, for evaluating the hundreds of recipes we received, and for entrusting us with their heirloom china, crystal, silver, and linens, we salute the following people:

Nancy Aaron
Ellen Aiken
Sara Stonesifer Airheart
Lelia Carson Albrecht
Lysa Mowles Allison
Brenda Barksdale Atkinson
Becky Dickey Austin
Margaret Ann Ewart Ayers
Cary White Baber
Susan Lazarus Bailey
Alison Rutherford Baird
Mary Catherine Ewart Baldridge
Kathryn Shipley Barrows
Jennifer Barry Baucom
Cynthia Oakey Bays
Susan Ellett Beaver
Mary Annis Belden
Anne Buford Berkeley
Katherine Collins Bezold
Vickie Holt Bibbee
Jennifer Wood Blackwood
Susan Wright Blaylock
Karen Boro-Godfrey
Joyce Uldriks Bowman
Shannon Meredith Brabham
Trudy Vandergrift Brailsford
Jessica Anne Brim
Fordham Baldridge Britt
Suzanne Martin Brown
Susan A. Bulbin
Carolyn Fletcher Bullington
Catherine Johnson Bush
R. Elizabeth Held Bush
Jane Ogden Butler
Mary Blair Ormsby Byrd
Constance Aikman Caldwell
Martha Call
Barbara Camp
Tina Wild Camp
Anne Stone Campbell
Christiann Caldwell Campbell

June Wall Camper
Mary Jane Carr
Sharon Webb Carroll
Nancy Kathleen Carson
Sandra Gannaway Carson
Katherine Brownlee Chambers
Jane Daffron Cheadle
Pamela Peacock Clark
Elyse Colette Coleman
Nan Lou Coleman
Mary Elizabeth Rainero Coles
Brandon Ring Comer
Julie Bishop Comer
Paige Leech Comer
Alison Ashby Conte
Suzanna Monroe Cory
Jennifer Cotner
Jane Eggleston Coulter
Anne Baldridge Cox
Carol Kemp Crawford
Wendy Conner Cummings
Anne Caddell Currin
Lynn Matthews Davis
Robin Dearing
Mary Robertson Delaney
Barbara McKenna Dickinson
Rebecca Short Doughton
Frances Brown Douthat
Kelly Stevens Douthat
Sharon Glaize Duckwall
Lynn Atkinson Elder
Lucy Russell Ellett
Kelly Huffman Ellis
Kimberly Carr Enochs
Elizabeth Mowles Erwin
Sally Darragh Ewart
Juliet Matthews Felts
Suzy Schwarz Fink
Fink's Jewelers
Sibyl Norment Fishburn
Jeanne Puckett Fishwick

Rebecca Spaid Fitzgerald
Mrs. Richard L. Fleshman
Cyndi Phillips Fletcher
Jeffrey Randolph Fletcher
Rosemary Duffee Francis
Elizabeth Fulghum Frankl
Janet Dunn Frantz
Laurie Gore Gibbons
Eva Donahue Goldsmith
Mary Field Green
Tammy Herring Grove
Carol Croxton Guilliams
Kathryn Lamon Gurley
Heather Lynn Haddan
Marilyn Mullen Harriman
Sherri Shrader Harrison
Jane Engleby Haynie
Emily Erlandson Henning
Lori Heyman
Helen Roberts Hill
Kathryn Good Hoback
Frances Brooks Holman
Hotel Roanoke and Conference Center
Linda Knowles Houston
Patricia Howard
Paula Zubieta Irons
Linda Irving
Debra Cunningham Jamieson
Virginia Barton Jarrett
Stephanie Taylor Jefferson
Bonnie Greer Johnson
Lori Elizabeth Jones
May Meier Justice
Ann Kelley Kemper
Gena Feind Kepley
Lisa Anderson Kepley
Mary Elizabeth Youmans Kepley
Jacqueline Mullen Kinder
Pamela Dunbar Kreger
Ruth Ellen Duvall Kuhnel
Pat Lambui
Jennifer Woodhall Landry
Linda Lanford
Page Muse Langhammer
Sally Snyder Laughon

Gray Lyles Lawson
Lee Wicker Lazarus
Martha Nash Legg
Betty Hardt Lesko
Langley Hinchee Lester
Ann Stadiem Levan
Angela Carter Link
Ona Martin Litwiller
Alice Chatham Loftin
Elizabeth Hickam Lowen
Leslie Cochran Magee
Emily Wright Mallory
JoAnn Stadler Markley
Martinique
Ann Davey Masters
Abigail Manring McBrayer
Puppie Stein McCloskey
Gaye Gerringer McClung
Cynthia Kinzel McGraw
Wendy Wells Moore
Lori Meyerhoeffer Moyer
Jennifer Burress Murray
Leigh Ann Robertson Myers
Pat Nervo
Joan Castner Niederlehner
Elizabeth Stevens Norman
Kristen Carol Nunnally
Mitzi Baker Oakey
Kathleen Keith Oddo
On The Rise Bread Company
Ann Peterson Orem
Carol Kambury Orndorff
Betty Brooke Morris Parrott
Martha Field Parrott
Doug Patterson
Gail Palmer Penn
Anne Phillips
Tracey Ellen Pirkey
Kimberly Stevens Pooley
Anne Marie Shoemaker Poore
B. J. Fitzgerald Preas
Provisions Gourmet
Mary Stewart Putney
Lori Lenart Rakes
Kitty Butterfield Ramsey

A Starry Salute

continued

Nancy Anderson Revercomb
Amy Louise Garswell Reyer
Nancy Stout Richards
Karen Sue Richardson
Marcia Brown Ridenhour
Patty Riester
Nancy Bolt Robertson
Mary Catherine Robey
Susanne Roderick
Kim Shaffner Roe
Ann Elizabeth Rohde
R.S.V.P., Limited
Katherine Baldridge Rurka
Kit Willis Rutherford
Virginia Moomaw Savage
Denise Wingo Scothorn
Virginia Thomas Shackelford
Vickie Nichols Sherertz
Martha Davis Shifflett
Chera L. Sink
Gene Hurt Smallwood
Robyn McNeece Smeltzer
Babs Kummer Smith
Lucinda Durham Smith
Lutheria Harrison Smith
Natalie Lynn Smith
Elizabeth Stacy
Lisa Dockery Stanley
Mary Stuart Cooke Stanley
Vickie Whitt Stauffer
Ann Garver Steadman
Elaine Eller Stephenson
Gari Dickson Stephenson
Anne Lee Stevens
Ann Kelly Stevens
Katharine Donahue Stevens

Amanda Story
Lori Greenspoon Strauss
Ellen Stroud
Judy Collins Stroud
Sumdat Farm Market
Diane Wallace Swann
Martha McKenzie Teague
June Barber Tegenkamp
Elizabeth Hobbs Thomas
Julie Thomas
Leigh Blakely Thomas
LuLu Pobst Thomas
Shari Brown Thomas
Susan Leftwich Thomas
Kimberly Denny Thompson
Tracey Lynn Thompson
Carobeth Trampe
Sara Huff Tuck
Mary Jane Mills Vanderhill
Virginia Museum of Transportation
Helen McHenry Vogel
Caroline Wallace
Jane Inge Wallace
Carolyn Lenz Warner
Carol Rust Watson
Fayetta Pittman Weaver
Jill Clerc West
Julie Habel Wheeler
Kristy Folger White
Marilyn Johnson Williams
Betty Cooke Winfree
Susanne McCarthy Wiseman
Tamar Turman Wood
Sandra Smeltzer Worthy
Jenny Lou St. Clair Wright

Index

Order Information

The Junior League of Roanoke Valley, Virginia, Inc.

541 Luck Avenue, Suite 317
Roanoke, Virginia 24016
phone: 540-343-3663
fax: 540-343-5512 • e-mail: jlrv@rev.net

Please send me _____ copies of Oh My Stars! at $24.95 each $ _____

Virginia residents add 4.5% sales tax $ _____

Postage & handling for first book to each address $3.50 each $ _____

Additional books shipped to same address $1.50 each $ _____

Total $ _____

_____
Name

_____
Address

_____
City   State   Zip

_____
Telephone   Fax

_____
e-mail

Method of Payment: [   ] MasterCard   [   ] VISA

_____
Account Number   Expiration Date

_____
Cardholder Name

_____
Signature

Please make checks payable to The Junior League of Roanoke Valley, Virginia, Inc.

Photocopies will be accepted.